The Co

Effect

LANCE MANLEY

&

DIANA ANGUSTIAS

ACKNOWLEDGMENTS

Diana Angustias

Adrian Reynolds

The American School of Tampico

Don Alejo Garza Tamez

The people of Tampico

QUOTES

"You will not fear the terror of night,
 nor the arrow that flies by day,
nor the pestilence that stalks in the darkness,
 nor the plague that destroys at midday."

— Psalm 91

"Be strong. Live honorably and with dignity. When you don't think you can, hold on."

— James Frey

"When you have nothing to lose, because everything you have has been taken away, all you have left is your voice, to claim for justice."

— Diana Angustias

Foreword

Lance

I went to the city of Tampico with my Mexican girlfriend (now ex) in November 2010 to stay with her family and teach English. Alarm bells began ringing on the first day when, after my jet lag had subsided, I suggested going for a jog.

"You can't. The drug gangs will know you're a tourist and kidnap you for ransom."

I laughed but was assured this wasn't a joke.

The people I met in Tampico were friendly, hard working and generous.

My ex girlfriend's family in particular showed me a lot of love and kindness during my stay there.

I heard and read about the violence in Tampico but never experienced it first hand. Stories were always "somebody said" but gradually the "somebody" became people I knew personally.

Adrian Reynolds taught at the same school as me and his brief prologue in this book is one of hundreds of examples of the brutality people had to endure if they were unlucky enough to get in the way of the feuding drug gangs.

Twice I received text messages while teaching to say "don't take the bus; we'll pick you up after work. Gun fight 2 blocks from you."

As we drove home we'd see car showrooms with bullet holes in the windows and once, puddles of blood in the road.

Diana Angustias is the mother of one of my former students from my time teaching English in the city. Her eldest daughter was in my class and was a happy, bubbly 12 year old girl who never failed to cheer everyone up.

The story involving Facebook that Diana tells at the end of this book is a perfect example of how in the UK we have a lot less to worry about than people whose daily lives are under threat of being ended violently.

In England it is a disciplinary offence in most educational establishments for a teacher to be friends on a social network with any student under 18. In Tampico, they have reality to worry about.

While I knew the situation in the city was bad, it's only through talking to Diana and reading her notes that I now know just HOW bad.
I never saw a gunfight, I never met a zeta.

I worked next door to the TV station where the severed head was thrown through the front door.

 I lived round the corner from the flyover where the four people (including a 14 year old girl) were found tied, gagged and hanged (the photo on the front cover).

However, both events were months before I arrived.

When the supermarket called H.E.B opened a new branch opposite my house, the mayor of Tampico attended the opening ceremony. We woke up to find about 16 heavily armed and masked soldiers outside the front gate.

A further 40 were further up the road. Protection, in case the zetas decided to kidnap him for ransom.

Amusingly one of the soldiers asked my ex girlfriend's mother if he could buy some firewood from us (while holding a very big machine gun and wearing a black balaclava with spare ammunition strapped to both legs).

I come from a country where not even the police are routinely armed.

Every day I'd see patrols of both soldiers and police. They drove in jeeps, with a tripod mounted machine gun on the back. I had heard that an army patrol stopped a car containing five young men.

They searched the vehicle, found a hidden bag of guns and shot all five of them dead. They then threw the bodies into the back of the jeep and left.

Another teacher from my school said that he was driving to work when he came across a firefight between bad guys and the police on Hidalgo Avenue (Tampico's main road).

Grenades were being thrown and there was a body spread-eagled in the road. He did a U-turn and phoned to cancel his lessons that day.

Three weeks before I came back to the UK the army forcibly took over one of Tampico's main police forces.

They were so corrupt that they couldn't be trusted anymore and were all sent home and replaced with soldiers.

As you read what Diana has to say remember that in most fiction even evil has standards.

Darth Vader loves his son.

Hannibal Lecter hates discourtesy and keeps his word.

Even Tony Soprano has a conscience.

The world Diana shows is one of fear, brutality and greed. Where there is no compassion and evil is pure and simply evil.

However the spirit and dignity of Diana and her family and friends shines through. It has been a privilege to put the book together and to those I met in Tampico and shared time with, my love to you all.

Lance Manley- November 2013

Prologue

Adrian Reynolds

Los Pinos restaurant, a Saturday night in June 2011, about 9.00pm. Me, wife & daughter, her cousin (plus new Belgian husband & baby), American friend of mine & his wife, plus a friend of my missus - quite a group, sitting by the window that looks out to the front.

I'm looking at the menu so I don't see it beginning, but I hear my American friend say, "Oh shit!" and dive for the floor.

As I look up, I see three guys (no masks) carrying military style weapons (AK-47s, probably) running in, calling to each other, as we all scramble for the deck.

The Bad Guys (Los Malos) are here.

On the floor, half under the table, I hear the Bad Guys calling to each other, "Check the kitchen!", "Check out back!", "Get that other motherfucker on the floor!" etc, etc.

I am aware of them beating the guy on the floor, demanding to know where his accomplice is (who, it seems, was not in the restaurant).

There's a strangely ordered sense of resigned panic, as though many have gone through this before.

I can hear a woman sobbing, crying, "Please don't hurt my children" and a Bad Guy shouts at her, "Shut the fuck up, you stupid bitch! We're not the zetas, we don't hurt women and children!"

Great, I think, so it's the Cartel del Golfo who are holding us at gunpoint - at least they are 99% for sure not interested in robbing us.

Out of curiosity (and feeling no fear, strangely, for I was on Prozac at the time), I look up from the prone position to see if I can see anything. I see a man spread-eagled, bleeding - presumably the one the Bad Guys were after.

Suddenly, there's a sharp thwack to my left shoulder and a growl of, "Get down, you asshole!"

I realise that the Bad Guy outside on point-duty, at the window opening, has seen me trying to peek and whacked me with the butt of his rifle.

Only later do I realise how lucky I had been. Were they zetas, he probably would have just pulled the trigger, no real need to aim with the business end of an AK just a few inches from my skull.

More shouting as they get the beaten guy to his feet. Backing out, frog marching the beaten one to the door, a Bad Guy shouts, "Nobody fucking move or call!"
I begin to pray that they do not bother to hose the place with automatic weapons fire as they leave for, being a wooden building, we would surely all be killed or maimed.

But they are gone and only later do I find out they had barricaded the street at both ends to ensure a clean getaway.

So, it's over - seemed like eternity but probably less than four minutes.

There are a few moments of stunned silence then the restaurant patrons begin to get to their feet, some moving quickly to the door to get out and away. It's over, and we survived.

Patrons are lighting cigarettes and drinking strong liquor to fortify themselves.

The owner is going from table to table, apologising fulsomely, ensuring all are well and offering free shots of tequila.

The mood eases, but most have left and the restaurant will close early that night, without explanation.

Diana
1946

My father told me once, the way people did justice, in the neighborhood where he lived when he was child.

He lived in a place called "El Cascajal", (stone chipping) it is by the Panuco River, in Tampico, and it is still known as a dangerous place. This land didn't exist at the beginning of the 20th century.

Tampico was the most important port in Mexico in that time.

Oil had been discovered, and in 1903, The Mexican Petroleum Company of California had drilled 19 oil wells, but it wasn't until 1904, when they were able to find a well with a production of 1,500 barrels per day.

In 1908 Sir Weatman Peerson a British man came to Tampico and after some attempts, he finally drilled a well that produced 2,500 barrels per day after discovering a belt of oil so rich that it was called "Faja de Oro" (Golden Belt).

The economy improved, and soon other foreign oil companies invested in Mexico. Downtown had beautiful French style buildings, and Tampico used to be known as "The Mexican New Orleans". Despite all this luxury, just a few blocks to the east, by the Panuco River There was El Cascajal.

It was a swamp, a place where nobody wanted to build up their homes. So people with no resources began to live there. The houses (actually, they were shacks) were built with wood, and on pillars, because usually were affected by floods.

As time went by, streets and lands were filled in with junk.

Stone chipping, but mainly with oyster shells, my father used to say it gives a strange scent to the whole neighborhood.

People who lived there, were usually working class; drivers, laborers, maids, bricklayers, and fishermen. But there were also pickpockets, whores, and burglars.

It was a muddy and overcrowded place, but everybody knew each other, and usually mothers used to go work knowing that their kids would be all right.

There were non-written rules for pickpockets, whores and burglars, the main rule was "Don't work in your own neighborhood, don't mess with your own people".

And everything went well for a few years.

Violence was not on the streets, it was at home. It was very common to listen to couples arguing at night, and sometimes, a man hitting his wife. But in that time, they used to think they were "private business" and even if they liked it or not, nobody did anything.

Everything went well, everybody followed those non written laws, and people felt protected in El Cascajal, until Tito grew up.

Tito was the only son of a single mother; they lived with his grandfather, who was a corrupt police officer.

Probably his mother tried to compensate for him not having a father, and allowed him do everything he wanted. Or maybe, the neighborhood corrupted him, who knows? But he became a burglar, addicted to marihuana and heroin.

Everything began slowly.

First, he used to take money from his mom's purse. Then, he began to steal from drunken men in the street. He used to choose the ones that were so drunk they were not able to fight back. It seemed easy. Everybody knew it was him, but they thought he would stop some day.

He didn't.

Next thing he did, was break into the houses, and snatch bags from the hands of women. People talked to his mother, but at this time she was unable to make him stop.

Tito went to jail a few times, the first time, his grandfather helped him to get out, but later, he did nothing. "He deserves it" he used to say.

But as they were misdemeanors, and his mother used to get money to pay bail, he used to spend just one or two nights in there.

It gave him a sense of power. He thought no one would be able to stop him. Until he took his grandfather's gun, and tried to rape a girl, after he had stolen her money.

He did not rape her, because in those neighborhoods, families were big, so, there were always dozens of half-naked and barefooted kids playing everywhere. A group of kids got to the place where he was with the girl, and he ran away.

That was the last thing that people from Cascajal could stand.

Men at El Cascajal had meeting. They were pissed off with Tito. It was enough, someone had to do something. They talked with his grandfather, he knew everything about his grandson, and told them he would talk to him. He would make him stop.
By this time Tito was out of control, he didn't listen to his grandfather and they fought.

As Tito was younger, he beat his grandfather easily, and once again, ran away with the gun.

Next morning, Tito´s grandfather led a meeting with the men. All of them would make him stop. First, they had to know where he went, what he did, who was with him, etc. every movement. So it was easier to catch him. They chased him for some days, until, one day, they got him.

It took four men to subdue him. But once they did it, he was put in a sack, taken to a house which had very high pillars, and hanged there, upside down.

Most of men whose families were attacked or stolen were there with bats and sticks.

Tito had his head covered but he knew every one of them because of their voices. But the men were not worried; actually, they were glad that he knew exactly who was there.

My dad was among the kids who witnessed when he was hanged upside down.

Men ordered him to get out of there, but they just went far enough away to not be seen and to not disturb, yet they were able to see what was going on.

His grandfather told Tito "We told you to stop, we asked you to leave, now, and you are going to know what happens to the guy who messes with his own people."

They took turns to beat him with the bats and sticks, in every beat, there was a reminder of everything he´d done.

"This is because you took my money", "This is because you broke in my house", and so they continued until it was the turn of the grandfather.

He beat him three times. "This is because you took my gun.""This one is because you hit me." and the last one:

"THIS IS, BECAUSE YOU MESSED WITH THE PEOPLE OF YOUR OWN NEIGHBORHOOD!"

They didn´t kill him, it was just a terrible beating and some broken ribs, but it worked, because he left Tampico and didn´t come back for at least 15 years, until people who had beaten him died.

It also worked as a lesson for other burglars; they didn't mess with their own people.

Diana

The Cartels

Cartel del Golfo is maybe the oldest criminal organization in Mexico. The headquarters are in Matamoros, Tamaulipas, a border city. This cartel began importing alcohol illegally to the United Sates in the 1930s during Prohibition.

It wasn't until the 1970s when, under the rule of Juan Nepomuceno Gerra, they focused completely on drugs, especially cocaine. Later when he retired he gave control to Juan García Abrego. The cartel then had internal conflicts until Osiel Cardenas Guillen took control of it.

It has always been known as a very violent criminal organization which had participated in murders and frequently had problems with other cartels due to its intimidation tactics. They used to kill other mafia bosses to remain in power. After the murder of some important mafia bosses, Osiel Cardenas wanted to keep his leadership, and asked Arturo Guzmán Decena, a retired Army lieutenant for his assistance.

Arturo Guzmán conscripted more than 30 men who had deserted the Mexican Army, most of them from a Special Forces group the GAFE. The salaries Osiel Cardenas offered them were much higher than those they could have ever got in the Mexican Army.

They were assigned to be his personal bodyguards, their main goal was to protect Cardenas from rival drug cartels and the Mexican military, They were the armed group that did the dirty jobs for Cartel del Golfo and they became the cartel´s mercenaries.

GAFE was an elite group specialized in the use of sophisticated weapons and were trained in the United States, France and Israel, in rapid deployment, marksmanship, ambushes, counter-surveillance and intimidation.

As they worked so efficiently, they helped Osiel Cardenas to consolidate his position and they got more power and responsibility over the years . They organized kidnappings, protection rackets, extortion, secured cocaine supplies as well as trafficking routes and murdered the enemies of the cartel, often in a sadistic way.

Probably Cartel del Golfo didn´t murder or execute people by itself, but it doesn't mean they are not guilty. They didn't do it by themselves, because they had people who did it for them. They had hired soldiers.

As ex-military, they followed a very rigid hierarchy and regardless of the fact that they were working for Cartel del Goflo , they formed a splinter group inside the organization . All I can say in Cartel del Golfo's defence, is that Cartel del Golfo didn't mess with civilians.

Their got their name zetas after its first commander, Arturo Guzmán Decena, whose Federal Judicial Police radio code was "Z1", (zeta one) a code given to high-ranking officers. For Federal Judicial Police in charge of a city, the radio code was "Z", and they were nicknamed as the alphabet letter in Spanish, "Zetas."

By this time, Cartel del Golfo was already a criminal organization that had a very important presence at the north east of Mexico, mainly in the states of Nuevo Leon, Veracruz and Tamaulipas, where they had significant influence.

They also had (and still have) network connections in the United States, Central and South America, Europe and Africa.

They were successful because they were able to create alliances with local and national politicians. Cartel del Golfo used to pay bribes, or even finance some of the political campaigns, something very common during the years when Mexico was ruled by PRI (Institutional Revolutionary Party). We were ruled by PRI for 71 years.

The government used to look the other way, as long as the cartels were discrete, and gave them money. If some of the members were out of control, the Mexican government usually arrested some of them or made them disappear, and the cartel members usually knew it was time to calm down. It was an open secret. and it seemed to work for everybody.

The cartels were able to work freely, politicians got more money, despite the amount they already took from our taxes, with unfinished or ridiculously expensive projects.

People wanted to believe everything was ok, or that they were not able to do anything, because when someone tried to do something, the government usually made them disappear. As long as it did not affect people directly they usually did not complain.

What we never thought was that we, as a nation with our conformism, were setting the stage for a cancer that now is affecting our daily life. That cancer is called corruption.

It allowed them to have control over important politicians, as well as governors and chiefs of police in Tamaulipas, which helped them became one of the most important criminal organizations in Mexico and the world.

Police forces in Tamaulipas have one of the lowest salaries in Mexico, although it is the state with the highest violence rate. As a result of this I can understand why police officers do not want to expose themselves in their working days, and are highly susceptible to corruption by the presence of organized crime. But I truly believe it is wrong.

They do not only refuse to protect us, they do not investigate properly, and contribute to this chaos, intimidating victims, and informing cartels about investigations developing against them. National Public Security System (SNSP) demanded to the state authorities to create better paying programs for policemen, so they and their families can be supported if they are hurt or die in service.

In 2000, PAN (National Action Party) won the elections, Vicente Fox became president and things changed. Fox didn't make a pact with the cartels, but he didn't chase them either. The economy improved, for the first time in 70 years, there were no devaluations and interest rates reduced gradually, so working class people had access to loans, and were able to buy houses, cars and send their kids to college.

For the first time in decades, we had in Mexico a growing middle class. The external debt was paid, and Mexico was peaceful.

Probably some analyst would disagree with me. I am not a professional analyst.

I am just a normal citizen and I am writing my opinion from my perspective, looking through the eyes of my family, who lost everything twice due to devaluations.

After PAN won the elections, my dad and husband, who are contractors, were able to work continuously without any problem. When we were ruled by PRI, they didn't get their payments on time, and their contracts were cancelled 6 months after the elections, and were activated another 6 months before the elections. They usually had problems to keep their company running and had to get loans with a really high interest and sell the company vehicles or tools to keep the company going.

In 2006, PAN won again, and with a steady economy, Felipe Calderón focused on combating the open drug trafficking in Mexico. Too many people think that Calderòn is responsible for the violence we face today. They only see the worst of two evils. They are not able to see that the problem has been there during the last 70 years.

The truth is that Calderon is the only president brave enough to face drug cartels. Probably, his strategy was not the best, and corrupt politicians, as well as the division in Cartel del Golfo didn't help.

I do not think that making a deal with cartels is the right answer. Cartels were already there, everybody knew it, but people preferred to look away, as long as cartels did not mess with citizens. We were in our comfort zone, and every time people participated paying bribes, or voting for a candidate because, "the party gave me $500.00" contributed to it.

Calderon only took the lid off, all the shit was already there.

The body is as the head is. But it is necessary to remember that if we are in a democracy, we are the ones who choose the head.

We are responsible for our destiny, in a personal and national way. We have what we want. Kids aspire to be like the people they admire, the most powerful or the strongest.

In a country where a drug dealer has more power and is more popular than a scientist or an athlete, kids wanna be drug dealers.

And some parents encourage them to do it. Later on they complain about violence, but they allowed it. As a society, we all allowed it at some point. If we do not learn from history, we are doomed to repeat it.
In 2012, most of the people voted for PRI. (I didn't!) Here we went again.

On March 2003, Osiel Cardenas Guillén was arrested, and the organization was partially ruled by Jorge Eduardo Costilla Sanchez. Its headquarters were still in Matamoros but it also included all the little towns around this city and the beach, Playa Bagdad.

Osiel Cardenas was taken to a high security prison, in Almoloya, near to Mexico City but he continued as the head of the group (in Mexico, if a prisoner has enough money, he is able to get a lot of privileges in jail) until his extradition by the American Government, in January 17, 2007.

This extradition wasn't executed immediately, because Osiel Cardenas still had to go through some prosecutions in Mexico.

In 2008, Heriberto Lazcano Lazcano was identified as the new head of Cartel del Golfo. His closest colleagues are Jorge Eduardo Costilla Sánchez, Antelmo Lazaro Rodríguez who has the nickname of "El Chamoy" and Antonio Ezequiel Cárdenas Guillén. The National Drug Intelligence Center pointed that Cartel del Golfo had a crisis in the transition of power and faced a division.

Some versions say that zetas were so powerful that original Golfos felt threatened and tried to execute them. Zetas knew their life as mercenaries would not be very long, and just as any other human being, they wanted to save their lives. Some other version says zetas realized they didn't need to work for the cartel any more due to their power and self efficiency. Probably both things happened.

Other sources mention that the conflict initiated between them was started by Samuel Flores Borrego, a lieutenant of Cartel del Golfo.

He killed Sergio Peña Mendoza, alias El Concorde 3, a lieutenant of Los Zetas. Golfos had ordered him to leave the zetas and work for them. As he refused to, he was tortured and brutally executed. When Miguel Treviño Morales the leader of zetas knew it, he demanded to Cartel del Golfo that they hand over to him the killer. They just wanted to kill the murderer of their friend. The Golfos refused, and the war began.

Up to that moment, both of them Golfos and zetas) worked in a very low profile way.

There were murders and kidnapping, but they used to be only among people involved with the drug business.

On January 30, 2010, some members of a zeta group ruled by Treviño Morales, took and executed 16 members from Cartel del Golfo, releasing all the devils on Tamaulipas. There were now two distinct groups. The zetas and the Golfos.

Both cartels had formed alliances with other drug cartels in Mexico.

Zetas with the Beltran-Leyva cartel, Juarez Cartel and Tijuana Cartel. Golfos with "La Familia" a cartel that has a great influence in Morelia, and the Sinaloa Cartel, who used to be their enemy, creating a war, that began in Tamaulipas but went to every corner of Mexico.

Over the years, some of the 31 original members of zetas had been killed, and young men had been hired to replace them, forming a group that resembles what Los Zetas used to be, but fortunately, still far from the efficiency of the original zetas.

From 2008 to 2011 Los Zetas have been responsible for massacres and attacks on civilians and rival cartels, that led to at least 400 murders.

During 2009

National government authorized the import of cars from the U.S.A to Mexico, just by following some regulations.

My husband was invited to invest in these kind of cars, by a mechanic he knew. He thought it was a good idea. If he invested his money in the bank, he wouldn't get the same profit, and besides, he would been able to have the money available immediately if he needed to. And by investing it in the cars, he could get it back in a really short time. If the cars were damaged, the mechanic could repair them for a very low cost.

So, he allied with this guy and every time he did not have to go out of town for his job, he used to go with him to McAllen to buy the vehicles.

He did it during a year.

They used to travel and be together so much that I used to make jokes about it.

Suddenly, at the beginning of 2010 my husband stopped traveling with him, and later on he quit investing in cars, and didn't answer some of his phone calls. He told me, that the sister of this guy, had a boyfriend who was a zeta. During one of his trips, the mechanic told him that the guy had given him the money so he could invest in the car business.

But he also told him about the way zetas hire people. In Reynosa everybody knew who was a gangster and to which organization they worked.

They even identify their car by gluing on the back window a tape with a Z form or the letters CDG (Cartel Del Golfo).

To get a job with the zetas, they first had to pass a test.

The test was to kill a whole family, in their house, the family that Zetas had previously chosen for them. It could be a family they were interested in killing, or any family. A family with the bad luck to be in their way when they had an applicant to train.

After the applicant had killed the whole family (in the most sadistic and painful way) he had to stay in the house for one or two weeks, cutting them into pieces to make them disappear easily. Some other members of the organization, would bring him food, and drugs, to help him go on.

The applicant had to eat, sleep, and even shit in the same room where he was tearing the bodies to pieces. When my husband knew it, he obviously thought, "What am I doing here, with this guy?!!"

The mechanic was not a zeta, but he was too close to a zeta member. So he gradually began to distance from him.

A friend of ours, lived in Altamira, in the north of Tampico. In 2010, he was not a rich person, but a hard worker.

He had just got married, and as soon as he married, he invested his money in a house and a car with his wife. The car was small, not too showy but fast.

One day we knew somebody had stolen his car. He did what you are supposed to do when that happens; he went to the police and made a legal statement.

His mother in law worked as secretary in the police motor offices in the same city, and as I said before, that was the first corporation corrupted by the Zetas, so, my friend asked his mother in law to investigate a little, may be that way it would be easier to get his car back.

And they almost succeeded. His mother in law found out that the car had been stolen by a member of the zetas. That guy stole the car just because he liked it.

Once he had it, he used it to hijack someone, but the "work" went wrong, and the hijacked person died in the car, after being beaten.

The heads of the zetas didn't know about the car and the murdered person until my friend asked his in-law to investigate.

So, that created a problem for all the people involved.

The guy that stole the car was not ordered to do it, he did it on his own, because he tried to get some extra money.

So he was killed because he didn't follow orders.

My friend got a phone call, telling him, the place and day he would have his car back.

He was afraid, but he went to pick up his car. It was left on a lonely place by the road. It was in terrible condition. The seats were covered with decaying blood, making the car impossible to be cleaned to to be used again.

My friend and his family (wife, father and mother in law) were also threatened by the family of the guy who stole the car, they said the guy would be still alive, if my friend hadn't investigated. They had to move to the other side of the country immediately.

They quit their jobs, and packed just a few things, left their house, city and friends, to save their lives. I knew about this because my friend asked some money from my husband.

He didn't have enough money to move the way he did. You usually do not expect to have that kind of emergency.

He didn't come back to Tampico until a few weeks ago.

Diana

December 31st 2009

We were at home celebrating with our family, when a friend came to visit us. He was a friend of my nephew and in time, he became a friend of all the family. His name was Agustin. He was a traffic officer, about 26 or 27 years old. He arrived with three of his own friends, two of them were from Haiti. We continued celebrating and drinking until sunrise and then they left.

That was the last time we saw him. On January 12, Haiti was devastated by an earthquake, and I told my nephew to advise his friend to be careful. It seemed that being at my house on New Year's Eve wasn't very lucky. "Just look what happened in Haiti", I told him. I was joking, of course. By February, we knew he had been kidnapped.

I kept asking my nephew about Agustin for some months until he told me that his family had hired some private investigators and they said he was dead.

His body was never found, but the investigation pointed to the face had been taken by zetas, (probably he had asked them money to avoid a fine) and they had "disappeared" him.

In 2009 Tampico was a peaceful city. Sometimes, we met with friends for barbecues or to have dinner together.

There was a very active night life, and many new bars and dance halls had been opened in the last couple of years on the main avenues through the metropolitan area, which has three cities; Tampico, Madero y Altamira. Restaurant and taco bars or other Mexican food stands were open all night long. Some of them used to be open 24 hours a day.

 I could drive back home late at night, with my three kids and we were safe. My biggest worry was that we'd get a flat tire and couldn't get a taxi soon.

We had heard about violence in Reynosa and Matamoros.

Those cities are on the border with the U.S.A. and we knew they had always been cities with drugs traffic problems but now it was beyond the authorities' control. It seemed to be so far away from our city! I had relatives nearby, but they lived in Brownsville or McAllen, they were safe. So, we didn't worry too much.

On March 2010, rumours started about "things" that were happening in Tampico. Like shootings in neighborhoods we knew were dangerous; people disappearing; telephone extortions, zetas demanding money to let you work, etc. But still it all seemed so unreal, that most of the people didn't believe it. TV, newspapers, even politicians kept saying they were just that, rumours and we shouldn't worry.

But people close to us started telling what they had seen. That was the cockroach effect. It is similar as when you clean up your house from those insects, you may kill some, but most of them, run away to the next door house. Our government tried to clean up the border cities from the zetas, and they just ran away to the nearest big cities. Tampico and Monterrey.

The first corporation infected by zetas' influence was traffic police officers. Once a taxi driver told me that he missed a red light, and a traffic officer asked him to stop. The officer didn't ask him for the driver's license, he asked him his "card"

"Which card?" The driver asked him.

"The card that lets you work, the zetas' card."

"I don't have it. I don't know about it." So the officer drove him to the zetas' offices, and they told him he must pay $1,000 weekly.

If he didn't they know his address and they would visit him at his home. (They took a photocopy of his ID.)

If he tried to quit his job, he had to pay anyway. So he had to work extra shifts to cover the rate.

"Who could I report it to?" He complained to me. "The police officers were the ones who took me with them? I have no money to leave the city."

Taxi drivers in Tampico and Reynosa were compelled to use radios and cars to help zetas, by crashing to create a delay if the army were following them and also informing them by radio if they saw a troop moving through the city.

In Tampico, we had heard that the governor of our state, Eugenio Hernández Flores, had an agreement with the zetas.

Actually, that they had paid for his political campaign in order to let them "work" freely.

In 2007, Procuraduría General de la Republica, had confiscated almost 12 tons of cocaine in Tampico.

As Eugenio the governor had an agreement with the zetas, they made him responsible for this loss, and said he ought to pay for that money.

He didn't have that amount of money, so he gave instructions to the police to try kidnapping and extorting money from people to get it.

On an April morning, I left my mobile phone at home. When I came back I had 10 lost calls. They were all from my husband. That was very strange, he used to travel a lot, and usually called me once a week.

When I called him back he was hysterical, asking me if I was OK, and why I didn't answer sooner.

When he came back, he told me that while they were driving to Reynosa, (my father was with him) an armed troop from drug gang Cartel del Golfo had made them stop on the road pointing at them with guns.

They demanded their IDs, and asked them where they came from, what were they doing there and what did they do for living.

My husband used to drive a golden pickup Ram 500. Once people from the cartel checked they were not zetas they were released, with an advice on his pick up, they "suggested" to change it for another vehicle that was "a little less showy", or he could continue having problems.

During April, there is a fair in Tampico, we celebrate that almost 200 years ago Tampico was founded. There is a small parade that represents the original founders, and then the fair starts for two weeks.

It is really quite small and expensive, but it is fun going there with the children and riding the roller coaster or attending the concert and listening to your favorite singers.

A guy that worked with my husband came from Reynosa to Tampico, to spend his vacation with his family. He worked as a crew leader for a construction company and also helped getting all necessary tools and equipment for their industrial work, so he was always on the street. As they were in the foundation of the drug conflicts, he had been at almost in every shooting in Reynosa. When he came to the office I exclaimed laughing:

"Hey, get out of here! It is dangerous to stand next to you! The guys are saying that they just look at you and everybody wants to get down. You should go to get cleaned with a shaman."

In Mexico many people still believe that shamans can clean your bad luck away, using herbs like rosemary to "sweep" you.

He laughed too, and said to me, "Yes, but what I need is to get cleaned with cornizuelo" (some kind of acacia with really big thorns) "because my luck is terrible!"

He had come to Tampico to try and relax and had taken his mom and sisters to the fair, for Jenny Rivera, a country singer very popular in Mexico.

Just when the concert began, there was a shooting.

There were 18,000 people in the fair that night.

Everybody tried to run away, and people started pushing each other, some fell down, there were kids and babies crying on the floor, and people crushed them!

Everybody was terrified, and didn't know what to do.

When we started to speak, we were joking and laughing to cover our fear, but when Tavo finished speaking, there were tears in his eyes. "I was afraid," he told me "but I can handle fear. But more than fear, I felt impotent, frustrated. Those poor kids and babies! We were in a fair; it's supposed to be family entertainment!"

There are too many versions of this event, people still say there was a collective hysteria, and there were no shootings, but fireworks. He said he can recognize shootings, after listening too many times in Reynosa.

Some minutes before the stampede at the fair, there was another shooting in a nude bar called "Mirage". That bar is really near to the fair, and it belonged to Cartel del Golfo, so zetas got there and killed everybody, dancers, waiters, and a few clients.
Then they chased each other and ended in the fair.

The morning after the shooting in the fair, my husband took a taxi, and noticed that the driver had scratches on his arms. Joking he told him, "Guess your wife is angry. Is it?"

"No," he replied. "Last night I was in the fair, when the shooting began. I had two options, zetas or Juancho. So I decided I would be better with Juancho and the mangrove's roots scratched my arms."

The fair is held by a lake that is in the middle of the city. Its name is "Laguna del Carpintero" it is surrounded by mangrove trees and plenty of wildlife. Almost 100 alligators live there. The biggest one is almost 3 meters long. That one is called Juancho.

I am not very religious, but I am an active Baptist and I used to pray every morning, so I started praying for the guys too, (as I call my husband's workers). That's the only thing I could do.

Diana

2010

I met a young boy that for some unknown reason, used to be called "El oso" (The Bear) I never knew his real name. He used to work with my husband. When I met him, he was financially responsible for his house, and was only 14 years old, so he quit studying.

He married at the age of 17 and had his first son at 19. He still had to supply for his mother, sister, and now a wife and son. As he was not a permanent worker, it was not strange that we didn't see him around the office for months.

In 2010, some of my husband's workers saw him in a gas station. They began to talk to him, and asked him where he was working now.
He told them he was working as a "Hawk". His place was in that gas station, which is on Hidalgo Avenue.

El oso had to stay there all day, with a mobile phone, and call someone to inform about the army troop movements, or any other incident on an enemy cartel. He received $5,000 weekly for his services.

He told them it was an "easy" job, and the salary seemed to be very good. But El oso told them, that once in there it was really hard to leave. He began to work with them, because, he couldn't get a job for some months, (the local economy was weakened) and he didn't want to move to another city. He thought it would be OK if worked for them until he could get another job. But he was wrong. The gangs told him they would kill him and his family if he ever tried to give it up.

And it was not an easy job, some weeks earlier, another hawk, didn't inform on an army troop, and some gangs boys were caught. He was beaten until they almost killed him but he was so severely injured that he will spend the rest of his life in a wheelchair.

He cannot dress or even eat by himself. They didn't kill him to give a lesson to other hawks. Hawks were hired to be alert, not to waste their time.

El oso's friends suggested that he send his family away, without taking anything from his house, just with the clothes they had on, and then once he knew his family was ok he should leave too.

We never saw him again, we don't know if he was able to leave or he was murdered.

We use to pray every day at school before our classes started. We would meet in a classroom and sometimes, we would tell our problems and pray for ourselves.

One winter morning, (probably at the end of November or beginning of December 2010) during one of these meetings, the janitor told us that two of her nephews had been taken from their house that morning, around 6:00am.

It was a 14 year old boy and a 7 year old girl.
Their parents had left earlier to go to work. The kids used to be left alone at home for an hour, have breakfast, and then the boy used to take his sister to school, then he went to high school.

They were taken in pajamas and with no shoes. We prayed for the kids for two days, at the third day, the janitor told us that the kids had been found.

She explained that kids were taken from his house by a cartel to some place in the north, near Soto La Marina.

It was a desert, an empty field

There was another family they knew; their next door neighbors. It seemed that their neighbors worked for the zetas, and once the other cartel got them, they denounced that family as if they also worked with them. Probably they never expected that the kids were taken. Once in the field, I guess the neighbors felt guilty, and told the cartel they had lied.

The cartel guys told the kids they will witness what the cartel does, to the people who lie to them, and accuse innocent guys, and shot them in front of the little kids.

Then they released them, showed them the way back to the road, and ordered them to not look back. They walked some kilometers in the cold desert and with no shoes to get to the road.

Once there, no one wanted to pick them up, until an old man stopped by and took them to the nearest army patrol. It seems that we, as town folk, had lost our sensibility to people in need because we were afraid to get involved in gang problems.

Finally they got home, a little hurt but alive. As long as we knew, the girl was not able to speak for some months due to the trauma of what they had seen.

They were not able to move to another city, not even to another house, as they had not enough money to do it.

So they stayed in the same house, feeling it was dangerous. They were not bothered again, but it was hard to live there after the kidnapping.

Diana

2010

Like almost every Mexican family, we are a really big family; with almost 250 members and we are spread all over Mexico with some in the United States. In 2010, I knew about one of my cousins that used to be a marine. We always knew that there was something different about him. He seemed to be too mature for his age, what we might consider an "old soul".

Our families lived close together when we were kids and I do not remember him doing things kids used to do. He was always responsible, honest, and too respectful for being a kid.

One of my uncles' favorite anecdotes, is that a summer day, when he was around 10 years old, they took all the nephews and nieces to the beach.

We were almost 20 kids, and as the uncles and aunts were drinking and having fun, nobody was taking care of us, but him.

I guess we became too noisy and mischievous , as we knew the adults were not looking after us, so he got angry and told the aunties and uncles "why did you bring them here, if you are not going to take care of them, I wanna have fun too, but I've been looking after them, so please, do what you supposed to do".

In time, he studied to be a lawyer, (he was the only one in his family and finished college) and got a job in the marine as some kind of prosecutor.

I guess he was OK with his job until 2010. As soon as he knew how bad situation was, he sent his family away.

He has two kids and a wife he adores, but it was dangerous for them to be in Mexico. He also used to keep in contact with us, but by messenger. He did not want to have the phone number of any member of the family in his mobile phone in order to protect us.
Although he was not in Tampico, he kept us informed on how to be safe (as long as his duties as marine let him).

As soon he knew we were planning to go to a wedding in a place that was out of the city, he warned me, that gangs were breaking in private parties, to steal jewelry, cars and girls.

By the end of 2010, my father told me that my cousin was too upset, depressed and disappointed to continue. As a prosecutor, he had to witness and report every incident after firefights between marines and cartels.

One day, when he was developing an investigation after a firefight, he saw that one of the gang boys was still alive. He called for help, but as soon as the one in charge got to the place, instead of helping the boy, he shot him in the head. My cousin was astonished, and couldn't say a word, but guess his faced showed what was on his mind.

The one who had shot the gang boy said, "Why do you want him alive? He might go out and kill someone else, its better on this way. And besides, I just follow orders."

He tried to report it to his authorities, but he was told the same. It was really hard for him to match this reality with his own principles; his favorite line from Lawyer's Decalogue (for Latin America) was : "Fight. You must fight for the right, but the day you have a conflict between right and justice, always fight for justice."

A friend of mine, for his job, had a chance to talk sometimes with a member of the army (I do not know their military rank).

Of course my friend used to ask them how bad the situation was, and what was happening in the city.

They did not used to give too much information, just the necessary to take precautionary measures. But one day, they told him they had chased and shot two gang boys. They chased them from El Moralillo,at the south of Tampico, over Libramiento Poniente, toward the north (about 3 or 4 kms away from my house!!) but before they could get to the toll booth, they got them over a bridge called "Puente Chairel".

When they got to them, soldiers shot to kill them.

Some days later, the mom of the boys went to the military field and asked for the boys (I guess she knew what they were working on) and one of the lieutenants told her, "Oh, yes we got them some days ago, they are dead now, and we are not going to give you the bodies. We also know you have another boy that works for the gangs, and we are chasing him, you are warned now, as soon as we catch him, he is going to die too".

As a mother it should be really painful to know your kids are dead, it is against nature that parents survive their kids, but, it should be even more painful, knowing that they are dead because you failed to bring them up properly, and as adults, they took bad decisions.

Similar stories were heard all over the city. Another man whose son worked in the army, told us once, that they captured around 25 guys, from 18 to 23 years old. They were working for zetas, kidnapping people or taking care of them. Soldiers had been ordered to kill them. There were a women in the group, a young woman and nobody didn't want to shoot her

But the one in charge of them, came by and asked them why they didn't kill her.

-It is a woman.- they said.

-So what? You have to kill her anyway! Don't know who is gonna do it, but one of you has to do it.- he ordered, and left.

It should be hard when you have been told to respect and protect women, and suddenly you had to act against to what you have been told all your life, against your beliefs. Don't know who did it. If the son of that man who told me about it, or someone else.

But it had to be done.

And it was done.

Unfortunately, the army only capture kids, cannon fodder. They do not catch the heads of the organizations.

They are still free.

Diana

March 28, 2010

In Cuernavaca, Morelos, five guys went out with the uncle of two of them. They went to a restaurant and during the dinner, they talked about an incident, where a camera and a mobile phone had been stolen from them some days before, in a club.

They were Jaime Alejo, Juan Sicilia, the brothers Julio and Luis Romero, and Jesus Chavez, all of them in their early 20's. The uncle of Romero´s brothers was retired Lieutenant-Colonel Alvaro Jaimes and with them was Maria del Socorro Estrada, who was dating Lieutenant-Colonel Jaimes.

Alvaro proposed that the boys go to the club and demand their stuff.

As he had been in the military, he thought they wouldn't have any problem as he was still able to intimidate people with his presence.

But the men's club belonged to the Beltran-Leyva cartel.

And the men, who had stolen the camera and mobile phone, were corrupted police officers who worked for that cartel.

That combination was lethal.

Next day, the dead bodies of all of them were found in a Civic Honda, with their hands and feet tied with packaging tape. Their heads were also covered with the same kind of tape, that had suffocated them to death.

But, why was this case particularly mentioned through all the country? Through all over Mexico, things like this were happening every day.

It was different because Juan Sicilia, was the son of Javier Sicilia, a poet, essayist, novelist, and journalist in Mexico. He contributes to various print media such as the Mexico City Daily, La Jornada and Proceso magazine.

Javier Sicilia had the economic and social resources and also easy access to the media.

Probably the boys didn't know that the men's club belonged to the cartel, but the cartel and the corrupt police officers didn't know either. They didn't know that among the victims was Juan Sicilia.

This incident evidenced the corruption in every level of local government, and police stations. Corruption that we all knew existed, but that the national and local governments refused to recognize and correct.

Sicilia, immediately after the burial of his son, led a protest in Cuernavaca, and later, in another 40 cities in Mexico, with more than 50,000 people involved, under the slogan "Estamos hasta la madre". This expression is usually very rude. It is a popular expression that we usually use to say we are really tired and angry for a situation and express a deep frustration. It would be similar to say "We are pissed off". It is not common that people lead protests with this kind of phrases as their slogan, but I know that a softer phrase wouldn't be able express what we normal citizens want to say;" ESTAMOS HASTA LA MADRE! STOP THIS! DO SOMETHING!!!"

Sicilia gave a voice to all those people who had lost a relative or a friend during the drug wars, and whose demands of justice and peace hadn't (and haven't) been listened to. During one of his speeches, he made a special call to the Justice Department:

"I am not asking to stop this struggle against the drug gangs, I know it has to be done. But do it correctly. You are protected by your bodyguards. You leave us, normal citizens, unprotected. Do your job, show us that you are doing your job effectively, and show us that your high salaries were properly assigned. Do justice according to the law, and do so, to every criminal that is illegally protected under the structures of power or government.

Every day we listen to terrible stories that tear us apart, and make us wonder; How and where did we lose our sense of justice and dignity? Our Mexico, our home, is surrounded by greatness, but also cracks and chasms which expand by neglect. Complacency and complicity have led us to this dreadful desolation.

These cracks, these open wounds, and the greatness of our house, are what forced us to walk here, intertwining our silence our sorrows.

We tell you straight in the face that you have to learn to look and listen and do not forget all our dead.

There are those who evil and crime has killed in three ways: depriving them of life; criminalizing and burying them in mass graves; and an ominous silence that is not ours. We tell you with our presence this ungraceful reality that you, the political classes, governments and police forces have denied and want to continue denying. A reality that criminals, in their madness, try to impose on us, with the omissions and lack of interest of all those who have some form of power in government."

After three years, Sicilia's case has not been closed, but almost every person involved in the murders has been arrested.

It has been called Sicilia´s case, but as Javier Sicilia said, that night 6 more people died, not only his son.

We all know that criminals were arrested "quickly" because Sicilia has the resources.

He also said, "The murder of my son gave a face and a name to all the 40,000 people who disappeared in 2010, I knew that things were bad, but, it wasn't until my son was murdered that I really knew it was so bad."

Diana

May 2010

All this madness got to me. I had a Great Dane that died after its pups were born, so I took care of them, and used to take them every week to the vet. One weekend, I was coming back with the 11 pups and I decided it was time to take my younger son (aged 6) to get a haircut.

When I was leaving the hairdresser's with my son in one hand and a box with the pups in the other, I saw in front of me what I thought was a collision between two golden pick up Ram 500s (just like my husband's). I stared and thought "I might help as witness." I clearly watched one of the pickup turned left in front of the other to stop it continuing.

From one of the pickups there got out a man in his 40s, he looked a little astonished. Suddenly from the other pickup, got out 4 really young kids with some kind of rifles.

They were really young! They couldn't be older than 20 or 22!

Those kids were wearing suits, and didn't look as I would imagine hired killers would look. They surrounded the man, and at that point I turned around with my kid and my dogs back to the hairdresser's.

As soon as I got in I shouted, "Get down! There are men with guns outside, and they're going to start shooting!"

When I looked around my son was on the floor and he asked me, "Like this mommy?"

I realized there were no walls to protect us. There was just a big glass show window. I kept thinking, "What can I do? How can I protect my kid? How can I help that man? They have weapons!"

I watched everything as if I were watching a movie, I couldn't believe my eyes!

Meanwhile, people on the street tried to run away and hide wherever they could. Cars, taxis and buses, turned around the wrong way, or drove back.

They hit and kicked the man and then took him to the other vehicle with two of the kid assassins, (because they were just kids!!!).

They took one of the pickups and two took the other and they left.

All that took only 5 or 7 minutes. As soon as they left, I left too. I was really astonished! I couldn't believe it!

I had promised my kids some Chinese food for lunch, so I stopped in the restaurant and asked for it. But I was thinking, "It's not real, probably I am wrong. May be there were not rifles. It was a misunderstanding and it didn't happen."

When I was in the restaurant I began to shake and the owner asked if I was OK. I told her what I had seen, and she offered me some water. But I asked for a beer. Water was not ideal to calm my nerves!

I had to do some other things, but after the restaurant I went directly home. My two little girls aged 12 and 10, were there, and I wanted to be with them.

They were not alone, because my husband's office is downstairs and the employees were there. But this all happened 10 blocks away from my house!

Until that day, I was confident my kids could stay at home safely.

I can't avoid smiling when I think of small things from that day. How could I open the damn hairdresser's door if in one hand I had my son and in the other the big box with 11 Great Dane pups?

Why did I stop at the restaurant? I should had gone directly home! How could I drive, if I was shaking and I couldn't control myself? I can't remember if my son, said something on the way back home. I can just remember his face when he was on the floor and asked me innocently, "Like this, mommy?" Up to then, I hadn't witnessed anything.

Everything I knew, I knew it because someone else had told me.

Diana

June 2010

On the other hand, there is Marisela Escobedo, she was an important activist who was killed outside the state house in Chihuahua. She became an activist after the confessed murderer of her daughter, was set free on April 30th 2010.

Rubi, Marisela's daughter, was killed when she was only 16 years old. She disappeared at the end of October 2008. Women had been being killed with impunity in Ciudad Juarez since 1993, so, another girl disappearing was something "common" for the police department, and soon Rubi's case was lost among thousands of other similar cases.

As the police were unable to solve this case, Marisela began research by herself.

She was sure that Rubi's boyfriend, Sergio Rafael BarrazaBocanegra (and the father of Rubi's baby girl) had killed her. He had left the city, just after Rubi disappeared.

Marisela spent almost a year searching for him, until she finally found Sergio in Fresnillo, Zacatecas. "I have already tired to do your job, here he is, now it is your turn" she said to police officers.

Sergio was finally arrested, and taken to Chihuahua for the trial.

During the trial, Sergio confessed his crime; he had killed Rubi, burnt the body and later buried her remains in a dump. He even showed the exact place where it was. But surprisingly he was set free, due to the "lack of proof".

In 2010 Marisela began a protest outside the assistant attorney's office in Chihuahua, claiming the maximum sentence for her daughter's killer. The sentence was set aside, and a court found him guilty, but he was already a fugitive.

Marisela, once again, did research on her own, and found him in Fresnillo. The police went to his house, but he ran away one more time.

During the next two years, Marisela traveled through the country, went to Mexico City, where she requested a hearing with the President, Felipe Calderón, and with the former Attorney General; Arturo Chavez Chavez, but both refused to receive her.

She had interviews with some people in the Attorney General's office who promised they would find Sergio, but they never did.

In 2010, Marisela denounced to the media, that she had received death threats from Sergio, who now worked for the zetas.

She had been living outside the state house for nine days, with another 3 women, whose girls had been killed too.

"I am not going to move to another place, until my girl's killer has been arrested. I am not going to hide or run away, if he is going to kill me, he will have to do it outside the state house, for the government's embarrassment!"

On December 19, 2010, she was placing a sign on the state house bars, at she had been done every night, it said, "Justice, governor's privilege, Is there going to be justice for my daughter?" Suddenly, a man came to talk to her and chased her down the sidewalk and finally, he shot her in the head.

Some newspapers said that a few days before her murder, she had been in a political meeting, held by the governor of Chihuahua, holding a sign that said "Justice, politician's privilege".

That bothered the governor Cesar Duarte who even scolded her for this.

Two days after her death, her brother in law was taken by a group of armed people, and later, found dead, covered with a blanket, and with a plastic bag on his head.

Her family, and her grandchildren, went to an unknown place in the U.S.A just after the burials, and requested political asylum.

In 2011, a man was identified by police as the killer of Marisela, he was known as "El Payaso" (the clown) but Marisela's son said, that witnesses declared he is not the one who killed her.

"We should not forget that our governors are corrupt, and they are able to make guilt out of nothing."

"El Payaso" died in September 2011.

Sergio Rafael Barraza Bocanegra, died during a firefight between the army and zetas, in San Luis Potosi. With the death of these two men, The Attorney General's Office considers the cases of Rubi and Marisela closed. Probably the cases are closed, but there is no justice in it.

On March 8, 2011, during the celebration of International Day of Women, a commemorative plaque, to honor Marisela was placed outside the Attorney General's Office, in the exact place where her body fell when she was shot, but it was removed a few hours later by the state government. Probably because it was a reminder of their corruption and inefficiency.

On March 11, members of 15 non government organizations, demanded that the plaque was placed there again.

It wasn't.

On June 9, 2011, members of the Movement for Peace with Justice & Dignity, placed a new plaque to honor Marisela. Among the members of that movement, were Sicilia, who stated "If the government removes it again, it will be a crime, it is a citizens' mandate, it doesn't matter if our government wants it or not".

Diana

June to July 2010

In the next months the people from Tampico developed some strategies to help each other. As TV news or newspapers didn't say anything we used to send messages by our mobile phones if we knew about shootings, to help others and avoid the place where the shooting was.

Twitter also helped us. If we were at home, and there was a shooting nearby, you could post it on Twitter, so people could know about it and take the necessary prevention measurements. Some web pages were opened, like Blog del Narco, and Historias del Narco.

Those pages kept us informed about what was really going on not only in Tampico, but in Tamaulipas and in Mexico.

After some high school students died on the street or in buses during shootings, everybody began to take their kids to school.

It doesn't matter if they were in kindergarten or college, it was safer, and if "something happened" at least they were all together. We as teachers, were ordered by the School Supervisors to show kids what to do during a shooting, just the same way we showed them what to do during an earthquake or fire.

The words zeta, golfo, mafia and some other became unmentionable in public places. Though we never were ordered not to do it, We used to say "maña" instead of "mafia", "the ones of the last letter" instead of zetas, and "the bad guys" (los malos) to talk about any of them.

Officially there were no firefights, there were "incidents" or "events" and people were not cut in pieces or disappeared, the authorities said those were just rumours that were made to discredit the governor.

If you wanted to express freely your disagreement, you had better do it at home, with people you trust and the door closed.

There were rumours that if you spoke out in public areas, you were in danger of being beaten or taken. Rumours, rumours, just rumours. But firefights and kidnappings began that way, and we saw them come true. We took every caution, even if sometimes, it seemed too much.

This was not an official order because the government kept saying that "nothing was happening".

We practiced with them in the classroom to identify the safest place in their houses, (usually the bathroom).

It should be a place surrounded by double walls, because the bullets could go through some walls. (Can you believe it?!! Bullets could go through brick walls!! They could even go through two brick walls!!!)

They should crawl from the place they were in, and once in the bathroom lay on the floor, and wait for the shooting to stop.

We also taught them what to do if they were on the street and there were shootings. If they were in the car with their parents, they should lay on the floor of the vehicle, and if they were walking on the street, they should look for the nearest car so they could lay under it.

They shouldn't run as army was ordered to shoot all the ones who ran away from the scene.

We received e-mails from Cartel del Golfo, advising that we were in a war zone.

They said it was not their intention to mess with citizens, they were just taking care of their commercial area, and trying to clean it up from zetas. They showed themselves as friends of people, and citizens of Tampico with families and kids living here and that also were involved in this problem.

They were sorry about what was going on, but said it was necessary to make zetas leave the place.

They declared that Cartel del Golfo didn't extort or hijack or kidnap ordinary people, they only mess with the ones directly involved with their business.

There also said that to prove this they had been working the state for many years, without causing any problem and supporting the economy. Actually, they were supporting the army, but in their own way. There was even a phone number to report zetas to Cartel del Golfo or ask for a job with them.

Travelling everywhere was very dangerous. Hijacking, extortion and shootings continued on a daily basis.

Unofficially, once again, soldiers at checking points suggested the travelers do not drive before 6:00 AM or after 4:00 PM. Mexico is a big country, traveling by plane is really expensive , and there are no passenger trains. Most of the people drive or travel by buses to go from one city to another.

In 2010, if the trip was too long and took more than 8 hours, they had to stop at 4:00 PM and spend the night in a hotel.

My husband, who traveled a lot, was not able to come home every weekend. Trips became longer and more expensive with the time schedule imposed by authorities due to violence.

Buses stopped offering night trips, after some of them were attacked. There were no guarantee for the passengers. If they stopped, they were mugged, women were raped and male teenagers were taken. If they didn't stop, zetas would shoot them.

Almost 40 of the most economically important families in Tampico left, and the economy collapsed.

They closed their companies, fired their workers, took their sons out of the schools, and moved to the south of Texas.

The American School of Tampico, one of the most important schools in Tampico, lost almost 400 students.

Schools couldn't pay their teachers' salaries. They had to fire them or reduce their salaries, even though that is not legal.

People who transported kids to the school, had to sell some of their vehicles, because there were not enough kids to transport and also fired the drivers they had hired. People who used to work in the houses of those families lost their jobs. It was hard for them to find a new one.

The houses lost their value because suddenly there were too many houses on sale and the people who could buy them had left the city.

From the top to the bottom, everybody was affected economically. Fortunately, the school where I work, is in a closed and quiet street, so we received many kids because parents were looking for schools were their kids could be safe.

My husband kept traveling for his job and he was stopped several times, sometimes by people from Cartel del Golfo, sometimes, by zetas, and a few times by the Army.

All of them always pointing at him with guns and checking his identification.

When things got harder, he began identifying himself as just a worker, or the driver, but never as the manager of the company. He continued refusing to change his vehicle. He used to travel very often to the north, giving support and maintenance to natural gas line pipes from PEMEX, his job is not in an office, but in the field. The area where he worked with his team, was near Reynosa, in Tamaulipas.

All north of the country was affected by gang problems.

Organized criminals stole petrol sometimes from clandestine pumps and sometimes they made people in pump stations fill their petrol tankers by threaten them or beating their workmates.

I knew about a PEMEX worker who was beaten to make him fill two trucks with petrol. As if being beaten wasn´t enough, the gang knew his home address, and his wife and kids' names. He was told that if he did not cooperate, or tried to denounce them, they would kill his family.

After the "incident", they got some legal advice, and denounced the gang. Police physicians checked them and declared they had been beaten and they had not beaten themselves, they were afraid to be accused of fraud. All this process took some days. Next day they were beaten again by gang boys. Someone in the police told them that they had denounced them.

They didn´t continue and after a year of internal investigation PEMEX made the victims responsible for the losses.

Thank God they were not accused of fraud or having stolen the petrol. But to PEMEX it was easy. PEMEX didn't care why, someone has to be responsible. They were responsible for the pump station, so they had to pay.

They didn't lose their jobs.

They were suspended for six months, with no salaries. They are not able to denounce, due to they are still afraid, and besides, to whom they are going to denounce it? Who cares?

After too many workers either from PEMEX or contractors, were beaten or found dead on the pipe lines, the army used to go with them, so they could continue with the works. Contractors or PEMEX workers used to go to their sites escorted by 4 to 6 army trucks.

There were 2 or 3 army trucks leading the convoy, then the contractor's vehicles with the workers and another 2 or 3 army trucks behind to protect them.

Once in the working area, the soldiers spread around to form a perimeter, so the contractors could work. At the end of the day they came back the same way. They were protected during their working day, but at night, or on weekends the contractors were left on their own.

One day, when he was in Monclova, he wanted to watch a football game, but the city was too small, there were no restaurants with TVs and he didn't have a hotel room. They were staying in Monterrey that is just a few kilometers away and used to come and go every day.

As he had to wait for the workers to end their working day, he bought a portable TV.

Then he looked for a calm place and parked there to watch the game. As soon as he parked, he was surrounded by three pickups.

One at the front, other behind, and the last one on one side. They told him to get out of his vehicle. They pointed at him with guns (it was becoming something very common) and asked him what was he doing there.

He explained about the football game, but they didn't listen to him. They ordered him to go, and told him that they were the owners of that place, and he was not allowed to park there. The ones who parked there just did it to buy drugs or to sell them. And he obviously was not buying anything. His workers again suggested changing his vehicle. Once again he refused to do it.

Despite all the restrictions my husband tried to be at home every weekend or at least every 10 days.

But one weekend that we were waiting for him at home, he called me and told me he wouldn't come.

He explained that some drug boys crashed his pickup in the hotel, and that he had to stay there for three weeks until the vehicle were ready. May be I heard something in his voice, but I didn't believe him. I used to pray every day for him and his team, and something inside told me that it wasn't completely the truth. I asked if he was OK, and he told me that he was OK. Later I understood he didn't want to worry me.

Around six months later, I knew that while he was in Saltillo, some drug boys got in to his room and took him out violently.

When he was in front of his truck, they asked him who he worked for

He identified himself as a driver in a construction company, but they didn't believe him, because his vehicle was too "showy", just like the kind of vehicles the mafia used to drive and besides, the plates were from Tamaulipas.

They crushed his pickup with a bigger truck, against the wall, and threatened him that if they saw him again in Saltillo, they would kill him.

Then they beat him and left. The receptionist had told them the room where he was. He wasn't safe at all in his room.

It took him almost three weeks to recover enough to travel back home. He left Saltillo in another vehicle, with the help of a worker, and stayed in Reynosa until he got well enough to go back home, and avoid a deep impression on the kids. He tried to sell his truck but he couldn't.

By then, zetas were stealing that kind of pickups, due to it was cheaper and safer to steal them to commit a crime and then leave it anywhere, than buy a new one.

Normal citizens tried to sell their pickups and trucks, because it was dangerous to drive them, but nobody wanted to buy big fancy pickups, and so prices went down and most of the people who owned this kind of vehicles kept them parked at home.

It had been a terrible investment to buy them.

As I said before, we were in a war zone, things got worse as days went by zetas began to hijack physicians and nurses from the street, even students of medicine, to attend to their hurt members.

So they stopped dressing in white.

That's the way they recognized them. As teachers we used to dress in white too for flag ceremonies, until the principal told us that it was dangerous because zetas could confuse us with doctors.

A friend told me, that she had spent the night in the emergency room of a well-known and prestigious hospital, because her mother-in-law was sick.

During that night, a woman came by, holding a little girl in her arms, shouting for help. There was a firefight outside, and the girl had been hurt. As soon as the doctors and nurses in E.R. saw her, they ran...away, to hide inside the hospital, leaving the woman with the receptionist.

The daughter of another friend, was studying medicine in the state university. She told us that three of her class mates, had leased a house because they were from another city (in Mexico, universities do not offer places to stay) One night, they woke up because somebody, was knocking the door insistently. Still asleep one of them opened the door, and immediately eight young men and another, a little older came in. They had different kind of rifles and weapons, and one of them was hurt. He had a bullet wound in his abdomen.

They told the students they would kill them if they tried to escape. Ordered to bring them alcohol, water and some towels, asked if they had some pain killers to assist the injured man. Then the students were locked in one of the bedrooms but first they took their laptops and mobile phones.

We assume they were zetas, because Golfos, as a organization already had their own doctors and safe houses who take care of them when they are hurt. And Golfos, usually do not hire very young people.

Next Morning, they left, taking the hurt guy with them. The students stood another 30 minutes in the bedroom, until they thought it was safe to go out.

The sofa and towels were blood stained and there were weapons and bullets left in the house. When the students saw the weapons, they thought that zetas could come back, so they left the house immediately, just with the clothes they had on.

Once in a safe place they made an anonymous call to the army and reported the incident. They never came back to the house, not even to pick up their personal belongings.

Fortunately, the gangsters never realized they were all studying medicine.

We lived in a semi urban neighborhood, there were just five families living there, by a federal road and a lake 500 metres behind our house.

When we got there, we thought it was a paradise.

We were just 5 minutes from the commercial area and 20 minutes from downtown. We even raised chickens and got a sheep! It was the perfect combination of both urban and rural worlds. The kids used to play on the street, explore the lake and observe wildlife. At the beginning the noise made by trucks didn't let us sleep, but in time, we were able to sleep without even noticing it.

When the drug war started, I didn't let my kids go to the lake, then, they were not able to play on the street, just in the yard.

Trucks stopped passing by at 9pm, and we didn't hear any kind of vehicles until sunrise. It was dangerous to drive on the roads. Just two kilometers to the north of my house, they used to steal cars and kidnap people.

I didn't feel safe at home. My husband decided to build our house as a cottage, with walls of brick and a wooden roof and the fence was some sort of corral, something very unusual in Tampico.

The windows didn't have bars, (every window in Tampico has bars) and there are two French windows, one in the living room, and the other in my bedroom. Both of them overlook a terrace.

I felt that everybody could get into my house. I'd heard that it had happened in other semi urban neighborhoods. Those houses were perfect for them to hide and rest for one or two nights. In the morning then they left after killing the owners and sometimes raping and killing the women or girls.

 I begged my husband to put bars in the windows and build up a stronger fence, but he refused to. He argued that if we did it, we could catch the zetas' attention.

So he suggested we move to another house.

But we couldn't move to any house, we had to check that the neighborhood were safe, and the house should have a big yard, because we had three of the pups from my Great Dane, and they were really big dogs. Also there were no leasers who would accept us with the dogs.

We also discussed moving to another city, but our parents didn't want to move, they are old now and need special attention, so we couldn't leave them alone. I have family in the United States, and I would like to send my kids there, but the girls didn't have passports. Their father, my ex-husband, didn't want to authorize it. He didn´t visit them or provide for their expenses, just his way to get revenge. So we decided to stay.

At the beginning I was afraid to leave the house, I wanted to stay there.

I wanted to believe it was safe. We didn't go to church or for a walk for a few weeks and just used to go to the school and back home immediately.

But a friend told me that we couldn't stop our life.

He was right, so, we left our life in God's hands, and continued with our routine. As my husband kept travelling, I felt alone and helpless at home.

I couldn't sleep and looked through the window every time the dogs barked.

One night I was in bed with my husband and I felt relaxed enough to read a while. A truck passed by the house, making a lot of noise, it sounded like a machine gun.

I turned to see my husband and he suddenly jumped out the bed, and tried to get under it. I held his hand and told him, "It's ok, it is only a truck, we´re at home." I guess he was still asleep because he just stared at me, and got back into the bed.

I laughed, (it was funny) but I also wanted to cry. I hadn't realized how stressed he was too. Next morning we talked and laughed about it.

I told him my fears and he replied, "Diana, why do you think you'd be safer with me at home? If gangs want to get in to the house, they will, it doesn't matter if I am here or not." He was right, but somehow, I felt safer when he was at home.

The school year finished and my older daughter went to High school. She has always been in private schools, but I decided to enroll her in a public high school near the house.

As a public institution, English lessons were basic; I also decided to enroll her in the A.T. S of Tampico, an English school, so she could continue learning and practicing English.

It was 20 minutes from our house.

As the girls also belonged to Las Gaviotas, a women's precision equestrian team , developing a discipline called Escaramuza, that is part of Charreria, Mexico's national sport
Tuesday and Thursday, we used to have a quick lunch and then leave the house for their practice at the Lienzo Charro. Then at 5 we left it for the English classes. My youngest one, did not practiced Charreria or study English, but as my husband was always traveling, he used to go with us everywhere we went.

Once in the school, my daughter went into the classroom, and we waited for her on the patio while my other kids did their homework. We did this for 10 months.

I was afraid to be on the street with my 3 kids. So I always drove looking everywhere.

As if I were paranoid, the radio – if I ever turned it on – was very low, and so was the air conditioner, so we could listen if there were shootings.

I didn't want to leave my daughter in the school.

I was afraid that something might happen and I wouldn't be there to protect her! The school was near a local TV station, where gangs from Cartel del Golfo had left a dead body by the door and thrown the severed head through the doorway.

One night that we were near A.T. S on the way back home there was a storm and suddenly we heard a very loud noise and strange blue light illuminated the whole street.

We all jumped from our seats, and looked around trying to find the source of the sound. My youngest daughter threw herself to the floor of the car, crying and yelling, "It's a grenade, it's a grenade!"

My other daughter started laughing hysterically.

My son just stared at me with wide eyes.

I was frantic trying to leave the place as soon as possible, the easiest way, trying get my crying daughter calmed and looking around to check if there were zetas or Golfos chasing someone. All at the same time this happened. It took me minutes to realize that the sound was thunder and lightning. As soon as I knew it, relief made me laugh, but I was angry too. It was insane, that my kids were reacting that way. Up to then I had tried to keep our life as normal as I could, I had hidden my fears, and tried to make feel my kids they were safe. It hasn't worked at all, my kids were stressed too.

Months went by, and violence continued in our city. I had only seen the hijacking of that man in May but I made the kids sleep in my bedroom. I wanted to be close to them if there was a shooting.

I couldn't stand to imagine that someone would break into the house and I wouldn't be with them immediately to protect them.

Every night we moved a mattress to my room, and two of the kids slept there, and another in my bed.

Sometimes, my husband called me and warned me about a shooting near the house, his friends in Tampico kept him informed. We used to turn the lights off and sleep in the living room as it was safer than in the bedrooms. One night I woke up with the sound of grenades exploding somewhere in the city. It seemed that the whole city was quiet because the explosions seemed to be far from my house, but I could hear them clearly.

At the beginning of 2010, there were traffic officers at almost all traffic lights.

However, after some of them were shot, and then a grenade was thrown at the police station, you couldn't see any in the city.

If there was a car collision, you had to wait 3 to 4 hours so they could come. They used to get to a collision very fast, trying to get some money, by intimidating people. (Cowards! They are paid with our money, with the taxes we pay, and when we needed them, they just disappeared!)

Golfos were chasing them because they helped zetas. I guess that after too many years of corruption, it was some kind of Divine Justice.

In August, there was another shooting in the main road of Tampico, Hidalgo Avenue.

It was in the commercial area, in front of Ihop restaurant, and involved local police and gangs.

Those were the last days of the summer vacations and my son went to spend the night in the house of our friend who has a son the same age.

It was not the first time that he did it, but that night, around 9:00pm I felt a little anxious.
I was reading in my bedroom and looked at the clock and thought, "It is bed time and he is not at home, I am not gonna kiss and say goodnight to him!" Then immediately I said to myself, "Why am I anxious? He is ok! It is not the first time he stays in his friend's house, don't be overprotective and paranoid now!"

I had never been worried before, when he stayed in his friend´s house. Next day I knew that there was a firefight at the same time I was thinking about kissing him goodnight.

It seems that some gang boys (guess they were zetas) were in a restaurant called Friday's and gangs from another syndicate (Golfos) tried to catch them in there. So they chased each other through some blocks around the place. At that time, my son was in a convenience store two blocks away from the restaurant.

They went there to buy something to drink for dinner, when the shooting began. The father said that he heard the gun shots, and pretended that everything was ok. It seems that the kids didn't realize what was going on. So he took the kids to the safest corner in the store, and invited them to choose whatever they wanted, distracting them from the noise that was outside.

It seems it worked, because my son didn´t remember it.

They were there around 40 minutes. As soon as they could go, they did. I don't know how he could get out them of there, the firefight lasted more than 40 minutes. I can only believe that God was with them.

A married couple who are friends of ours were just near the Ihop during the firefighting. The wife told me that her car was used as shield for some gang boys that were chased by the army.

The gangs were in front of them, and the army behind the car.

None of them wanted to give up, and pointed their guns at each other with my friends in the middle. She tried to leave the car, but her husband didn't let her. He held her hand and made her stay inside.

"I wanna get out! Let me get out of here!" she yelled.

"If you go out, they will shoot you," Her husband replied.

"They will shoot us anyway in here!"

Suddenly some cars moved and there was enough space so the gangs ran away.

My friends also left immediately.

The Escaramuza teacher of my girls, was in the house of her sister, just at the back street of Friday's when the shooting began.

Her sister had a high risk pregnancy and both were overweight women.

They were just with their kids. One has a girl aged 5 in 2010 and also a baby boy, her sister also had a boy, that was 2 or 3 years old. When they heard the shots, they tried to hide in a really small cupboard.

"I don't know how we got in there," she told me. "I am 75 kilos, and my sister is still heavier with her pregnancy. We put the kids against the wall, and then we sat on the floor of the cupboard, trying to protect them with our bodies. I was also terrified by the idea that she could go into labor. If so, how could I take her to the hospital?"

She said that shots were terrible, but hearing the way gangs shouted each other was worse. It was not what they said, things like "I'm gonna kill you son of a bitch, I'm gonna spread your guts on the floor, I will cut you in pieces," but the way they said it.

Listening to their voices made her know how insane all of them were.

She couldn't leave her sister's house until midnight, when the army got there, they didn't allow anyone to get out or in the perimeter. A police vehicle was shot up until it burned. We could see the marks of the fire on the ground for a few weeks, and we still can see the bullets marks on a palm tree where the truck was.

An aunt has a friend that lives in the street where the firefight was and he told her that he was in his bedroom when the shots began and threw himself to the floor as soon as he heard them.

When the sound stopped, he stood up and looked through the window.

He saw that the army was on the street, picking up dead bodies and piling them up in a truck, if they found a gang boy alive, they shot him to kill him and threw him in the truck.

It was as if a garbage truck were picking up the rubbish bags. I have mixed feelings on this. On one hand, I guess they should be treated as human beings, but why do we want them in Mexican jails, where they can escape by tens any day, with the help of the authorities? If they are dead, they won't hurt anybody again.

As the school year went by, I began wondering if I had made the right choice when I decidedto enroll my eldest girl in the public school.

Up to that date, she had been a regular student. Most of her teachers used to say she was really smart, but it was hard for her be constant, finish her classwork and have good habits.

But once in high school, she used to skip classes or didn't go to school and usually lied to me.

She tried to justify her behavior arguing everybody in the school did the same.

I didn't used to believe we can be influenced negatively by the people or environment around us. I used to tell her it was her choice, her attitude.

I had studied in a public high school, and when I was a teenager the environment was healthy, and I innocently thought it was still the same way.

In October three men and a very young girl were hanged from a bridge facing McDonalds on Hidalgo Avenue.

The girl was only 14 years old, the same age as my daughter is now!

They were taken from a house near the state high school where my daughter used to go. We don't know if she was directly involved, or she was just in the wrong place at the wrong moment.

A homeless man used to live under the bridge, every night, when we came back from the English School we used to see him climbing the wall of the bridge to sleep in the space between the wall and the upper part of it.

He had a lot of stuff in there, but after gangs hanged the bodies, he disappeared. There are rumours that the gangs took him because he saw them. Only his stuff remained there for some weeks, until the local government removed it.

A few days after the people were hanged, I was talking about the young girl with my daughter, Elizabeth and pointed that the dead girl was only two years older than her. I also told her that I was really worried every day, thinking she might skip classes or leave the school, when the situation was terrible in the city. She stared at me and opened her mouth as if she wanted to say something, but she didn't. I asked her what she wanted to say, but she refused to talk.

We knew about dead bodies tied to a lamppost with barbed wire, and others left on the street, sometimes, in pieces, with messages from zetas.

Those messages were usually written with terrible grammar or spelling, that let us know the kind of people who were involved in gang life.

They were uneducated people, people that always had really low salaries, and now were dazzled by the money gangs offered to work with them.

However it does not justify what they were doing.

A friend had a chance to talk with the woman of one of them. She told her that they preferred to live only 3 or 4 years, but with a "good life style" than live 30 or 40 years working hard and in terrible conditions.

Diana

November 18th 2010

There was another shooting in Marques de Guadalupe Street. It was early in the morning, some minutes past 7:00 am ,the time when everybody is getting ready to go to school or their jobs. A van was coming from west to east, and just behind Tel-cel , and in front of Hollywood Park it was surrounded by three or four cars. From the cars some men got out, and shot the people inside.

Then they took some of the bodies and put them in the cars' trunks and left, leaving behind at least other two bodies.

Some friends live in front of the place where the shooting was, (actually the ones who were in their car between the gangs and the army) and a cowboy from La Herradura was passing by at the exact time of the shooting.

So they saw it all.

They told me that one of the cars had closed the way of the van and before they could do anything, shooting started. There was a woman giving orders about what to do with the bodies.

The men who got down from the cars were working in pairs, and were strong enough (or drugged enough) to take the bodies with one hand, while were holding rifles on the other, to put them in the boots.

They left because the army was coming and they could hear the sirens. As long as the witnesses could listen, it seemed they needed the bodies to get their fee.

As soon as the hired killers left, a man raised up from the dead bodies.

He was seriously injured, but walked at least 50 meters with a gun in his hand, and tried to stop a cab. Of course the cab didn´t stop. Witnesses said he walked toward Avenida Hidalgo, leaving a bloody trail and no one knows what happened to him.

Once everything calmed down, people who lived in the area went out of their houses to be sure everybody was ok. Two guys were walking on the sidewalk when the shootings began. As there were no place to hide, one of them, a really tall guy, So he curved around himself and managed to hide between a wall and a very big flowerpot. It was a really small space. They found him in that fetal position, still in there and helped him to get out. He didn't stop whispering, "I don't know how I could get in there, I don't know how I could do it."

The other guy, a teenager, dived in some construction sand that was on the side walk in a desperate attempt to be invisible.

More than afraid of being hurt accidentally, he was afraid to be killed or taken just for being in the wrong place at the wrong moment. He was found sat on the sand, cleaning off his face and clothes.

Some days later, we found out that the dead men in the van had broken into a house that was close to the lake, behind La Herradura.

They kidnapped the owners, a woman and her teenage son during the night. They took a bath, had supper, and changed their clothes (they stole some of the owner's clothes). Next morning they took the family car (the van) and asked the kid to drive it for them. Even though he was able to drive, he said he didn't know, they insisted but he kept saying he couldn't.

That saved his life.

By December 2010 I was exhausted emotionally, I had spent too many months without a good night of sleep, and I was falling asleep everywhere. We used to decorate our house with lights all over the roof for Christmas. But that year, we decided not to, for the attention. We nearly didn't buy a pine tree.

We, like all people in Tampico wanted to be discrete, invisible if possible for the zetas.

We didn't have our party for new year either, as we usually used to. We just spent the night at home watching movies and to went bed early. We weren't even sad for not having our party.

The situation in the city was so bad, that we didn't hesitate.

Diana

January 2011

It was time to register my girls to the Mexican Federation of Charrería, in order to participate in state and national competitions as juvenile Escaramuzas. In May 2010 we went to Cd. Victoria for the state competition as it was relatively safe to do it. But they didn't participate in the national competition 2010 because one of the girls fell off a horse and broke her leg two weeks before.

Registering the girls was a problem. If we registered them in Tamaulipas, to represent our state, we should go to Reynosa for their competition. By that time it was really dangerous traveling to that place.

We knew that zetas were not only after stolen cars and pickups on the road.

They also took the women they liked, sometimes little girls, raped and tortured them.

If the women were "lucky" they used to release them on the road after.

The Escaramuza teacher was also teaching in Naranjos, a town that is 3 hours to the south of Tampico, in the state of Veracruz. She told us that the team from Naranjos had said we could register the girls as if they belonged to that area.

That way, they could go to the south, representing Veracruz, not Tamaulipas. It bothered us.

We wanted to represent our state, but we didn't want to take any unnecessary risk. As a juvenile team they had a very good chance to get a good place. We decided to register them in Veracruz, so their competition would be held in Tuxpam.

In May 2011, We took all precautionary measures for going to Tuxpam.

We travelled in a group, each family in their own car, but following each other and keeping in touch by radio. When we were in Tuxpam that night, we couldn't believe that there was a nightlife.

It had disappeared in Tampico. People were on the street, walking, laughing, having supper in restaurants, it was amazing! We could be on the street without looking everywhere, in case there were zetas or golfos! As there was a carnival, we heard fireworks all over the city and we jumped every time we heard them! My kids used to asked me every day, "are there any shootings here, mom?"

They couldn't believe it either! Finally I could sleep. We really enjoyed those days in Tuxpam and nobody wanted to go back to Tampico. Once again, that made me realize how stressed we were. The girls won the first prize, so they could go to the national championship representing Veracruz .

Back in Tampico, the girls continued with their riding activities, and we used to meet in La Herradura with other teams of escaramuzas and charros. In one of those meetings, a saw a girl from the adults team who was unusually thin.

I had known her for some years and it was strange to see her that way. I talked to her and she told me that her fiancé had been killed some weeks ago.

He was a lawyer who worked for the state government.

He was assigned to temporarily cover the position of governor in Altamira's prison, due to the last governor quitting under the pressure of been threatened by zetas. He worked directly for the Governor of Tamaulipas, Eugenio Hernandez Flores.

In jail, there were some men that worked for zetas. He as a governor had been pushed to release them.

But, if he did, his image and career would be damaged. But if he didn't, his life was in danger. He had to travel very often to Cd. Victoria, the capital of the state, and visit the governor in his house.

As it was really dangerous to do the 3 hour trip, he used to do it by bus, hoping to be safer.

The day he was killed, he had traveled to Cd. Victoria, trying to get an appointment with the Governor, and ask him his advice on the problem he had with zetas.

As soon as he got to Cd. Victoria he sent a message to his girlfriend, and then when he got to the governor's house, he sent another, telling her where he was. He used to do it to let her know he was OK. That was the last message she received. She believes that he was taken from the governor's house.

She worked as manager in a bank, and her fiancé had an account in that bank. She knew approximately the time when they killed him, because there were vouchers on his credit card signed by him. It seems zetas drove him to different parts of town, made him take out money and finally killed him, leaving the body on a path.

"It was his signature," she said. "I could recognize it anywhere. The zetas never requested money from the family. It was not their intention to leave him alive."

Diana

April 23rd, 2011

During Eastern vacations the escaramuzas' families organized a barbecue for the girls at La Herradura, as a treat prior to their participation in the competition. Some families decided to spend the night there and brought some tents. As the violence had reduced our outdoor activities, we thought it would be a great idea because the lienzo is in the city, and really near to our houses, so we thought we would be fine.

There were at least 13 families in the party, but only 4 decided to spend the night there. The kids played and roasted wieners and marshmallows and around 12:00am fell asleep. The night of the barbecue, I had a terrible cold, so I decided to stay at home. I went to bed early, and fell asleep immediately.

I didn't wake up until next morning around 9:00am when my family got home. My husband asked the kids to clean up their rooms, and took me to our bedroom.

He told me that they had been spent the night by the lake, in a palapa that is close to the restrooms. They had a wonderful view of the city, and its main road, Hidalgo Avenue.

Around 3:00am they woke up to the sound of gunfire. They could see the bursts and for a moment didn't know what to do. They were really close. Suddenly everything stopped and as the kids didn't wake up, they decided to stay there until sunrise, hoping no one tried to hide in the lienzo. Later that day we knew that every car agency in Hidalgo Avenue had been shot as well as some supermarkets. Since then, we have never organized another camping party with the girls.

Diana

April/ May 2011

One day, in April or May 2011, I was in my classroom, with my second grade students. Kids from kindergarten were in recess time, when suddenly, the door was opened and the kids came in. My classroom was in the first level of the school, and it had two doors. One opened to the patio, and the other to a corridor that takes you to the principal's office and some other classrooms.

The kindergarten teacher smiled at me a little anxious and asked, "Can we come in?" I knew that something was wrong, but, I tried to disguise my fears. "Of course" I replied.

They passed through the classroom and went to the hall. Just a few seconds later, the principal called me to the corridor.

He told me that there was a shooting going on in the back street near the school.

We were surrounded by houses, and the school is in a closed street.

She thought it was not likely that gangs would go to the school, but stray bullets could be dangerous for the kids.

"Your classroom is surrounded by other classrooms, I think you´ll be OK, just don't let the kids go to the restroom. And keep calm. It is not necessary to ask the kids to lay on the floor" . We didn't hear anything, so we tried so that the kids did not notice anything strange, but we failed. One of my students asked me, "Why did the kids from kinder pass through our classroom? Is there a shooting?"

"No", I answered, "it is an emergency drill".

"It is strange", replied another, "We usually go outside during emergency drills. What kind of emergency is this drill?"

Guess I answered flood or tornado or something similar, there were too many questions!

My younger daughter (who was 11 years old in 2011) was in a classroom on the second floor, so they had to lay on the floor because their classroom had a high risk to get a stray bullet.

Later on, the teacher told me that she (my daughter) was terrified, and tried to get some protection by crawling under the desk. But once she realized the desk wouldn't protect her (it was made of wood) she began to cry. It was hard for her. And I was not with her in that moment!

I was worried about my kids, but I was more terrified that one of my students could be hurt.

If one of my kids were hurt or killed, It would be really painful to me, but they were mine! I don't have to give explanations.

With regard to my students, They were under my responsibility, their parents left them with us every morning in the school, expecting to pick them up at noon, hoping that we take care of them.

I knew I had no control over firefights but I couldn't avoid thinking over and over again, what am I going to tell to the parents if they get hurt? How I am going to explain to them? Fortunately, nothing happened. Well, that is a lie. It would be correct to say that no student was hurt. But something DID happen! Just a block away from the school, there were men killing each other.

THAT'S something.

In those days, the situation at home with my daughter was beyond my control. Teachers used to have meetings with me to complain about her behavior, she didn't finish her classwork or did the homework, and skipped classes. Though they said she was smart, her grades were really low. We used to argue all the time and our relationship was terrible.

I used to take her every day to the school trying to keep her safe, but she thought it was a way to control her. As I was not able to pick her up when she left the school due to my job I told her to go directly to my school as soon as she went out.

However, after the firefight near the school I was not sure it was a good idea. I didn't know what to do, and was always afraid she could be taken or get hurt in a firefight. Who is going to believe what we had been going through, if sometimes, I cannot believe it myself?

She had to walk 20 minutes to get to my school, and those 20 minutes were endless to me. I held my breath when my watch marked 1:20 then she left her school, and checked it every minute until 1:40, when she looked through the window of my classroom and waved her hand. Then, I felt my soul come back to my body and was able to breathe again

In 2010, a total of 15,237 people were killed in Mexico as a result of drug wars including civilians, police officers, soldiers and assassins.

One day, when we got home, my daughter Elizabeth told me that the father of one of her classmates was in prison. The girl was sad, she didn't know what would happen to her life, but also was worried about what would happen to her dad.

-Probably everything will be ok in one or two weeks, - I told her – Why is he in jail?

- Kidnapping a little girl. –she answered.

-Probably it is just a mistake and he will be free in a few weeks. – I said again. What..

But mom, -Elizabeth interrupted – my classmate says he did it.

I was astonished. She also told me that some of her classmates gave her instructions on who she should avoid, and how to behave in front of some of the students who used to bully students from first grade. They even told her which one of them could sell her drugs in the school.

That student was still in the school because there was no proof about it.

I was speechless. I tried to say something but only manage to open my mouth and close it again. Where the hell was my daughter??!! What a mistake I had made when I decided to enroll her in that school!! The school year was about to end, and I was not able to get a place in another school until next semester.

She had to finish it in that school.

After kidnapping and extortions, cartels began to kill "hawks" on the street. Hawks are the "eyes of the cities" for zetas. They are set in a place, usually a busy street, to inform and tell on military convoys or any other strange movement that may affect their bosses. They worked 12 hour shifts, and used to be at every traffic light, offering to clean your windscreen for some coins. It was funny, because people that used to work cleaning windscreens, were usually homeless and they used to get angry if you didn't give them a coin.

But suddenly, there were too many people trying to clean your windscreen, wearing very good clothes and mobile phones, and they didn't seem to mind if you did not give them money.

One night, around 9:00pm one of my cousins was waiting for the bus outside of Wal-Mart, in Hidalgo Avenue. He was standing next to a public phone, and on the other side there was a really young boy probably 17 or 18 years old, that used to work cleaning windscreens. It seems he was waiting for his bus too.

Hidalgo Avenue has 5 lanes. From the high speed lane on the left, without stopping, a car fired at the boy, who was on the sidewalk and killed him almost instantly. Everything was so fast and precise, that my cousin was not able to react. He didn't even throw himself to the floor. The boy was killed with just one shot to his chest.

My cousin took the bus and went home with an unreal feeling.

He did not try to help him, because he couldn't believe it.

He saw him die just in a few seconds after the shot. But he couldn't believe IT was real, until he got home. He began to cry but had mixed feelings.

He was happy to be alive; my cousin was standing right next to him!

He was also sad, as he worked in that area, he used to see the boy every day, so he had become someone familiar to him. He still wonders if the boy would have survived if he would have done something to help him.

We all think that it was almost impossible, but we cannot change my cousin's mind. There were some other murders in the city the same way in daylight. Ordinary people that seemed to be in their ordinary business were shot from a car.

A shoemaker, and a fruit seller that had his business near my mom's house, are some examples. Some people said they were "hawks", and some other said that they refused to pay the fee to let them work.

We really don't know and probably we'll never know the reason, but now they are dead, they are part of the statistics.

It makes me feel thankful to God because he keeps his promise in Psalm 91:7, "If a thousand fall at your side or ten thousand at your right hand, it will not come near to you."

My husband was beaten by gangs in 2010, but none of my family have been taken or killed.

We are still alive, and together.

Diana

A Sunday morning in June.

I got up early because I needed to dry some clothes I wanted to wear that day. I had left them in the washing machine the night before. When I opened the door to go downstairs, I heard what seemed an air conditioner on. I guessed I was still half asleep (it was 6:00am!) I turned around looking for the source of the noise, and saw a silver double cab truck outside the neighbour's house. The motor was on, and the windows were misted up. I couldn't see if someone was inside. I thought it was strange to have visits so early on Sunday, but I didn't care.

Later on, around 9:00am I went with the kids to church and my husband went to some other place.

When we left church at noon, my husband called me.

He asked me to go to my mom's house, he explained me that there were 4 trucks parked in the neighborhood, with at least four armed guys each, and another outside, by the road, apparently watching.

An old man that lives in the street behind us woke up early too and saw a truck outside his house. He was curious, so looked through the window and saw them.

They were asleep, and there were a lot of weapons all over the seats and floor. He called my husband and told him to keep us away from the neighborhood.

They didn't leave until the afternoon.

We came back to our house after sunset. We were afraid they could begin a firefight. I guess they only needed a place to rest. The neighborhood was perfect for them. Close to the city but plenty of places to hide.

At school, the principal read us one morning Psalm 91 and I clung to this verse with all my heart, with all my soul and with all my mind.

I made it my personal prayer. ("He will cover you with his feathers and under his wings you will find refuge; his faithfulness will be your shield and rampart and strength.") Psalm 91 gave me hope (it still does).

After swine flu, and later violence on our streets, it seemed to me that Psalm 91 would had been written especially for us Mexicans at this specific time of our lives. I used to read it every morning when I woke up, and thanked God for giving me another chance, another day.

At night, I used to read it again, and felt thankful that God let me end my day at home with my family, safe.

Two weeks later around 2:30am I got up because the dogs were barking a lot . My three dogs could be really noisy, every time they saw a rat, raccoon, or an opossum. But this time there was something different in their barking.

It seemed that someone or something had made them get really angry. I could also hear my neighbour's dogs barking the same way. I was worried because my husband had just got to the house a half hour earlier drunk, and I didn't want him to wake up.

I was still thinking about that when I got a phone call.

An uncle lived nearby and told me whispering, "Darling, there are men outside my house, I can hear everything they say, and they are waiting to shoot somebody.

If, you have the army's phone number, call them now! Then go to a safe place. If a firefight begins, our houses are on the bullets' way!"

I went back to my bedroom, woke up my husband and told him about the men. I had the army's phone number, but he took the phone from my hands and didn't let me call them. "If you call them, it would be worse. They could break into our house!" he said.

"But they could break in anyway!" I answered him.

We have to do something!

Suddenly, every dog in the neighborhood stopped barking. I tried to wake up my kids, to take them to the bathroom, but he didn't let me do it either. "I hope they leave soon without shooting," he said. "It is not necessary to wake up the kids and frighten them!"

I looked through the window but I couldn´t see anything. The dogs were quiet and I began to think maybe it was a bad dream. I sat down in my kid's bedroom and prayed. If it was our time to die, I was not afraid.

God could stop everything, but if we had to go through that, I accepted it. I knew our lives were not in our hands, but in His. All I wanted was that my kids do not suffer. I was terrified that they could break into the house and my girls would be raped. I begged God, that if we have to die, it would be quickly.

When I opened my eyes, I saw the rear red light of a car. I told my husband, "Somebody is leaving." Immediately the phone rang again. It was my uncle, telling me they had gone.

Next morning, we talked with my uncle about it.
They were also woken up by the dog barks and immediately realized that there were men outside the house, as the windows were open. My uncle was able to listen to their conversations clearly.

Gangs got instructions by walkie talkie to lay on their stomachs and get ready to shoot. The person or people they were waiting for, was in the north, towards downtown in the south.

They expected to him to go by the road in front of our house. But at the last moment they took another way through the city. They received the order to meet him in another part of the city.

Early in the morning, my cousins got out of the house, and checked the place where the gangs had been.

They found some bottles of Gatorade, a lot of bubble gum packs, *(they wanted to keep fresh breath?!!)* and bullets, big bullets, the same length as my index finger. My uncle told me, laughing that every dog in the neighborhood seemed to feel aversion to the men that got in that night, by the way they barked, but also, that dogs were smart enough to stop barking, and look for the safest place as soon as gangsters got their guns ready to shoot. Dogs in that moment didn't want to mess with guns.

We had a neighbors' meeting due to the fact it was the second time that they got into the neighborhood. My uncle and us wanted to place a gate, to limit the access to people that do not belong to the neighborhood, but other neighbors didn't agree. They were afraid that gangsters could get angry and take revenge. So we didn't do it.

From that moment on, I didn't let my kids get out of the house. Not even in the yard or the balcony, if there were a firefight, it would be really dangerous, because there were no place to hide.

I used to live especially worried about my girls that now were young ladies. I knew about girls that had been taken from the street, and even though sometimes their parents were with them the parents were beaten and couldn´t do anything.

One day the school secretary got to the office crying. She told us that two classmates of her daughter had been taken from the bus stop.

They were waiting for the bus to go college, when a van stopped by and some men made them to get in.

Nobody did anything. Once again, people were afraid to get hurt. Up to date, nobody has seen them again. The mother refuses to go to sleep or turn the lights off at night. She argues that her girls may come back some day, and she wants to be there. Can somebody imagine the way she feels? She said that if her girls were found dead, at least she would have a place to cry. A place to go, where she'd know that her girls are. But with no bodies, it is harder to be in mourning.

But boys were also in danger, a workmate told us that zetas were now taking boys from low class neighborhoods, forced them to consume drugs, and when they were already addicts, zetas made the boys work for them, and controlled them with drugs.

One of her cousins had been taken that way.

They know he was still alive, sometimes they saw him, but he refused to talk to them and it was obvious that he was on drugs and was too afraid to speak to them or too high that he didn't even recognize them anymore.

Diana

November 15th 2010

On November 15th 2010, we woke up with amazing news. This time it was commented on by TV, radio and newspapers. A 77 year old man had died defending his ranch from zetas.

He was Don Alejo Garza Tamez.

Don Alejo, was born in Allende, Nuevo León, a state close to Tamaulipas. It is a woody place, and his father had a sawmill , where he as well as his brothers used to work since they were kids.

He also used to hunt in the forest close to his father's sawmill and it became his passion, he hunted deer, doves and geese. Soon, he became famous as a hunter and for his marksmanship and had a wide collections of weapons for legal hunting and sports.

When he grew up Don Alejo opened a wood yard in Monterrey, and later, had branches in some other small cities near Monterrey. On November 13, 2010, 4 men from the zetas visited to demand that he give them his property. They gave Don Alejo 24 hours to leave it or he would be killed.

They already had an agreement with a notary, who would send him all the necessary documents to give them the ranch "legally". (something very common in 2010).

"I'll give you nothing", he replied, with the diplomacy of a gentleman.

"And I will be waiting for all of you here!"

Everybody knew he was a man of his word. His word was worth more than a signed contract.

Everybody knew it, except the zetas.

The ranch house is located 23 kilometers west on the Linares- Ciudad Victoria road, in Güemez, Tamaulipas, by dam Vicente Guerrero. He had bought this property with his brother when they were young, later on, they divided it, and his brother kept the area close to Corona river. It has easy access to both states, Tamaulipas and Nuevo Leon.

When the zetas left, he paid his workers their salary, thanked them for their work and loyalty, and ordered them to go away from the ranch and not come back. Don Alejo spent all that Saturday gathering his weapons and bullets, and developing a strategy to face the zetas.

He placed weapons on every window and door in his house and waited quietly, all night long, until they came. The night was probably eternal for him, but he was a professional hunter, so I guess he had enough patient and courage to do it.

On Sunday, November 14, around 4:00 am almost 30 zetas came to the ranch and parked in front. There were almost 30 men, firing into the air and shouting they would take possession of the property. Probably they expected no problems, maybe an easy surrender, and that any people in the building would come out terrified with their hands in the air.

But things were very different.

Don Alejo fired back and soon, every man outside the house began to shoot at him.

When the army got to the ranch, some hours later, the air smelled of gunpowder. The house was partially destroyed by the bullets and grenades and when soldiers got in, they expected to find many people in there. With the evidence, the army was able to reconstruct the scene.

Don Alejo alone had repelled 30 zetas.

Everything indicates that zetas fired on him several times, and even though he was severely injured, he continued firing back. It was only by throwing grenades that they finally stopped him. But he had already killed 4 men and injured 2, that were found unconscious by the soldiers. Finally the zetas left because they knew the army would come to that place and they couldn't stay there. Don Alejo's body was torn apart by the grenades

He became a national hero, representing the indignation and frustration we all had for being helpless.

After his death, finally the army began to patrol the roads.

There was a moment during 2010, when an uncle asked me if my husband and I had a strategy in case some of us were taken. We didn't , we hadn't thought about it at all, always expecting not to be kidnapped.

But he was right, we should have had one.

At the beginning, my husband didn't want to talk about it. You usually do not think about it until it is strictly necessary.

We finally agreed, that if one of us was taken, we would not pay. To pay would encourage them to continue kidnapping, and there were no guarantees we would be released alive.

But when we tried to decide what we would do if one of the kids were taken, we couldn't continue. We have not been able to end that conversation up to date. I really don't know what I would do if that happened.

Diana

Summer 2010

After the second time that gangsters were in our neighborhood my husband had installed an alarm system. He still refused to place bars on the windows or build a good fence.

He supposed that if somebody broke into the house, the alarm would send a signal to a central office and police would come if I do not disconnect and give a special code to the operator. I didn't want zetas to get into my house but I didn't want police officers either. I didn't trust them.

On June 29, 2010, the gubernatorial candidate Rodolfo Torre Cantú, was killed in Soto La Marina, with another 6 people that were traveling with him.

He was on the way to the airport to take a flight that will take him to Matamoros, a border city where he would close his campaign. As surveys was in his favor, he was considered virtually the governor.

It happened 6 days before the elections. Once again, we think zetas wanted to show who was in charge in the state.

From that moment the government of the state couldn't keep saying that nothing was happening, but, still help didn't come.

It took at least another 10 months for the army to take over from the local police, and begin patrolling the streets.

When Rodolfo Torre Cantú was murdered, Eugenio Hernandez Flores, the governor at that time, and Oscar Perez Inguanzo, Mayor of Tampico were not living in Tamaulipas anymore, everybody knew that they had their houses at the south of Texas, they only used to come when it was strictly necessary, by helicopter.

They didn't land in the airport, they used to do it in Club de Regatas Corona, a club by lake Chairel close to downtown, trying to expose themselves as little as possible.

It was frustrating, we were this way, because of them!

They let zetas rule Tampico and Tamaulipas yet they did nothing to stop them and now they just left us with all this mess.

They both had stolen our resources, the money of our taxes and ran away to buy their houses in Texas. Some years later, a trial was held against them. But they were released, "because of not enough proof."

At some point the army were always on the streets, we could see three or four trucks full of soldiers with heavy weapons.
I had mixed feelings on it. Finally we were receiving help! On one hand, I wanted to believe that they were there to protect us. But as other authorities had already left, or had been corrupted, it was hard to believe. On the other hand, I was afraid to be close to them, because if a firefight begins, we could be hurt.

At school, there were kids whose parents were soldiers, or marines.

One day, I talked to one of the parents, about the guys that had been in our neighborhood. He told me, "Don't be afraid of us, we are here to help you, you should call us. When you denounce them, it is anonymous.

Nobody is going to take revenge on you for this and you help us and help yourself to stop this"

Sometimes they used to stop us and check our vehicles, as I had nothing to hide, I was not afraid to be checked, but I was afraid to be shot just for being close to them.

When I left the school with my kids, every day, I had two ways to go home. In one way I had to pass by the military field. I used to avoid driving by there, because a grenade had been launched there by zetas some day in 2010, but one day I just forgot it, and went home that way.

I was driving in the low speed lane, and there were another three vehicles behind me, and another one to my left.

Suddenly, we heard the sirens and I could see in my rear mirror that three or four trucks with soldiers were coming.

They tried to leave us behind, but the car on my left couldn't change to the right lane, because we were there. So I decided to speed up a little for the other vehicle could to let them go. As soon as we did it, the trucks sped up too, but when they were in front of me, they shot in the air twice, and then, pointed their guns at us. I stopped, and so did every car behind me. I was more surprised than afraid. "Why have they shot?"I thought. "Well maybe they are looking for someone in one of these cars."

I raised my hands and looked around, as people in other cars did the same.

The soldiers didn't stop, they just left, but continued pointing their guns at us. In the afternoon I knew that they were on the way to help in a firefight. Probably they were afraid too. They couldn´t know who were ordinary people and who were zetas.

During some weeks, while I was at home, I had seen too many soldiers in trucks patrolling the neighborhood. It made me feel a little anxious. There had been trucks with soldiers before, but not so many like now.

One night I was at home with my kids. It was around 8.00pm and we just had finished dinner. I was washing the dishes and my kids were watching TV.

At home, the living room, dining room and kitchen are in a big rectangular room with no walls to divide the area.

Suddenly we heard like if fireworks were ignited, but somehow it was different. My older girl stared at me and asked, "Did you hear it? What was that?"

"I don't know, but why don't you lock the door?" I replied.

As soon as she did it, the shots became stronger. My three kids stared at me and I told them, "Crawl to the bathroom and stay there!" I'll never forget the face of the little one, he was shocked when he was crawling to the bathroom, but he didn't cry.

While they did it, I ran to the door and checked it was locked, set the alarm on, and turned the lights and the TV off. Then I joined them in the bathroom. "Our aunt!" my daughter told me. "Would she know about it? Why don't you call her?"

So I left the bathroom, took the phone and called her. Her house was on a back street but she hadn't heard anything.

She took the phone and went to the bathroom too with my cousins.

When I hung up the phone I could hear someone shouting, "To the floor! Do not speak! I told you to lay on the floor!"

I felt relieved. They were not swearing or boasting they could kill someone! It was the army vs. drug boys! It was less dangerous than drug boys vs. drug boys. At least, I knew there were less possibilities that gangsters broke in our house. But I was afraid anyway. I called my husband who was practicing in the lienzo, told him about the firefight and asked him not to come home until I called him again.

At one point, we stopped hearing shots, so I came out of the bathroom and looked through the window.

I could see the street full of soldiers, and occasionally heard some more gunshots.

My dogs! I thought, (yes it is probably amazing, but I did it.) They could be afraid. I left the bathroom, opened the door, and called them in a low voice. My husband had sold one of the three Great Danes, so now we only had two and one of them is half deaf.

The first one that came upstairs, was the one who could hear. I let her in and closed the door. Almost immediately, the other one came upstairs and scratched the door.

I opened it and let her in too.

I felt a little safer with my Great Danes inside the house. I guessed if someone broke in the house, they would help me to protect my kids. The firefight lasted almost two hours. Two hours we spent on the bathroom floor, that it is 2.10mts by 2mts. It was uncomfortable and cold.

There was a moment when I really wanted desperately to get out of my house and run with my kids to the lake. I would like to hide them, make them disappear. I wished they could be somewhere else but not in there, at that moment! I wanted to cry, I knew I was about to lose control and I couldn't. If I did, the kids would be really frightened. Once again, I prayed. I had nothing to do but pray.

My husband had been calling me, and told me that he was near but soldiers didn't let him go to the house.

By 10:00pm the gunshots finally stopped. The army went all over the neighborhood with some kind of small war tanks, lit with really powerful lights.

Once they were sure nobody else was hiding, and everything was ok, they allowed people to go home.

Next morning we knew just half block away from home, there was a house that had been used to hold prisoners. The army knew it, and they were waiting for the right moment to proceed. It seemed they rescued some people, including kids.

One of kidnappers climbed the fence and tried to run away towards the road. But he couldn't get there. He got to an abandoned property 5 meters from the road, and hid in the bushes but the army followed him there.

There is a house next to the property, and the owners were outside. When the soldiers got there they ordered them to lay on to floor.

Those were the shouts I had heard. The soldiers shot towards the bushes, and injured him. He still tried to run to the road, but he was then shot and killed by the soldiers. He died 250 meters from my house.

It is funny, but after the incident in front of the house, we felt lighter and safe.
For at least another year, drug boys wouldn't consider our neighborhood as a good place to hide.

And finally my husband built a 3 meters high rock wall around the house.

Diana

December 2011

My youngest son was diagnosed with epilepsy, with manifestation of absent seizures and also had language disorders and immaturity in his fine motor skills. My older daughter had been diagnosed with ADHD so we spent our time with the neurologist, psychiatrist, and language therapist, and also with the girls' riding activities.

I didn't want to be on the street too many hours, but I wanted the girls to continue doing their activities. I felt that gave them a sense of normality to their lives. By the end of January 2012 I couldn't continue with my life, I didn't want to wake up in the morning. When I finally woke up, all I wanted to do was cry (and I used to do it!) I forgot everything and fell asleep everywhere.

I wanted to fall asleep and not wake up again (though I never had suicide thoughts).

I said to myself that I couldn't fall to pieces at that moment. I had too many responsibilities and probably it was just pre-menstrual syndrome. That is until I had to realize that it was NOT premenstrual syndrome. So finally, I went to the doctor. Too many months of stress had made me lose weight and I had a hormonal disorder that had taken me to depression. I underwent hormonal treatment for six months to overcome it and continue with my life.

We spent New Year 's Eve 2011, in Veracruz, with a sister-in-law, it was still safer traveling there. At 12:00am we gave a toast and hugged everybody, when fireworks began.

My son got panicked and begged us to take him to the bathroom.

He thought there were gunshots. We tried to explain to him but he didn't listen to us. He agreed not to stay in the bathroom, but refused to get out of the house.

He has overcome that now but that night we were sad, angry and worried.

In 2012, the state championship for escaramuzas was held in Tampico, so we were happy we wouldn't have to travel with the girls. Fortunately, everything was ok, and there were no incidents. For the national championship, the team had to go to Irapuato . At that moment, only my youngest girl was still in the team. We had a family party with my in-laws, and my husband couldn't go with us, so I would travel with one of the guys from my husband's office, my daughter and a niece.

Both girls were 12 years old.

There is a small town in the south of Tampico, that was now very dangerous.

Its name is El Moralillo and it is in the State of Veracruz. There is no other way to go to Irapuato other than going through it. The morning we had to travel, we woke up really early.

We had agreed with the members of the team, to meet in a specific place that is just 500 meters away from my house at 7:00am and travel all together.

Nine families would travel to Irapuato, 8 from Las Gaviotas (the team where my daughter was) and another one from the Segovia family.

They were in another team that wouldn't participate, but they wanted to cheer us on.

When we were ready to go my dad got home with some tacos that my mom had cooked for us. We had already planned to stop by the road for lunch, but we didn't want to offend my mom, and we delayed a little to eat them. It took us only 5 minutes, just 5 minutes.

I got an SMS from one of the parents, telling us that they were waiting for us. So we left the house around 7:05. To get to El Moralillo we have to go over a bridge that is called, precisely, Puente del Moralillo.

We were the first car in the line.

When we got to the bridge, I saw the Segovia family walking on it. I waved my hand surprised, and when Mrs. Segovia saw us, she waved too, with a mix of desperation and relief in her face.

I asked the driver to stop, but we couldn't do it on the bridge he had to drive some meters first. Every escaramuzas family stopped by to know had happened. They told us that their van had been stolen just 5 minutes earlier.

The thieves tried to take their 14 year old son with them, but she begged them not to do it.

Finally, they left them on the bridge with no money or mobile phones for asking for help. "They might be around, we should go it is dangerous to be here," she said. We had a quick meeting. We had to decide if we'd continue or go back to Tampico. We decided to go to Irapuato. It was dangerous, but we were tired of arranging our lives according to zetas.

One of the members of the escaramuza drove the Segovia back to their house, and we travelled as fast as we could to cross that town.

They met us again in the State of San Luis, for lunch and to talk about what had happened.

I cannot avoid thinking that if we hadn't delayed for lunch it might have happened to us. To any of us. Five minutes, just five minutes probably made the difference. They didn't have a fancy van so having an old vehicle did not guarantee anything. Travelling in group didn't either. Was there ANY way to be safe?

Gradually life in Tampico has returned to normal, or something similar to normal. There are still soldiers on the streets, and occasionally firefights. But there is night life again, and we are a little relaxed.

There are still murders. Just last month a nephew wanted to go to Altamira beach for fishing, and army had closed the beach because 10 dead bodies were found.

There were no evidence that they had been killed there, they were thrown into that place. Can you imagine, transporting 10 dead bodies and no one saw or knew anything? It is unbelievable.

News still do not inform about what is really going on. And people who used to inform on line, have been threatened.

The zetas offered a reward of $600,000 pesos for denouncing people who post news about them.

Some weeks ago, I was talking to my son about where and how I used to play when I was a child.

"Where did you hide during the firefights, mom?" he asked me suddenly.

"When I was a child, there were no firefights."

He stared at me for a long time then laughed and told me, "You are kidding!"

He still does not believe me. I don't know what is more infuriating. Is it that he doesn't believe me, or that this whole mess is now part of his life? It will be always in his memories.

My sister lives in Puerto Rico, and asked me why we don't leave. I guess, the first lines of the musical The Fiddler on the Roof answers that question perfectly.

"A fiddler on the roof. Sounds crazy, no? But here, in our little village of Anatevka, (Tampico) you might say every one of us is a fiddler on the roof trying to scratch out a pleasant, simple tune without breaking his neck.

It isn't easy.

You may ask 'Why do we stay up there if it's so dangerous?' Well, we stay because Anatevka is our home."

Diana

Chronicles of kidnappings.

There is a hardware store in Tampico, on Carretera Tampico-Mante, it is well known because it has been there for at least 30 years. Now it has become a reference point for everybody in the city. The owners are two brothers, that I am going to call Juan and Luis, and they were friends of my husband. As it is on a busy street, it was not strange that in front of it there were car collisions frequently. In 2011, during one of these accidents, they were outside witnessing what had happened, when a car stopped by and took Luis.

Juan tried to help him, pulled his brother from the hands of the kidnapers and fought them, some of their employees came outside to help them, but probably they were stronger, or well armed, and Luis was taken anyway.

Juan got in his car, and followed them with one of the employees for some blocks, until the kidnapers fired at them several times.

Finally Juan stopped the car, because he was afraid that his brother would be killed. There were motor officers outside the hardware store, because of the collision, and they saw everything, but they did nothing. They did not do a single thing. They didn't try to help, or call the army, they just stood there watching everything.

Some hours later, they got the expected phone call, asking for the money to release Luis and of course, ordered them not to call the police. But they did it. They called to police for help, and anyway, tried to get the money.

They were hard workers, not rich, so it took them some weeks to get it.

When they finally got it, kidnapers ordered that the wife of Luis hand over the money.

She was terrified, if she was taken, or killed, who would take care of her kids? But she also loved her husband, and wanted him back. They told them that she had to drive to the south, toward a town called Naranjos, in the state of Veracruz.

They made her drive alone, at night and they were calling to her mobile phone and gave her instructions frequently. There is a bridge after this town, and a path that takes you to a ranch. She was ordered to take that path, and drive in the dark until she got another phone call. She was told to leave the money on the ground, by a tree, and leave immediately.

Her husband would be released at a convenience store by the road. She drove back to the convenience store, and waited for her husband.

It was 3:00 am. She stood there until 10:00. By this time, her family thought she had been also taken. She didn't want to call her family until she had good news, but finally she had to face the truth; her husband probably wouldn't come.

Luis was never found dead or alive. Later on, they knew that a chief of the police office was involved in the kidnappings, and he informed the kidnappers that the family of Luis had contacted the police, so they think that Luis was killed as soon as the kidnappers knew the family had called the police, but the money was requested anyway.

Finding the body became an obsession for Juan. He hired some private investigators from the U.S.A.

They gave them a complete report on where Luis had been during the kidnapping and also informed them that the car collision was on purpose, to distract people in order to take him.

They even gave them the names and places where the criminals were. The only information they couldn't get, was where the body is.

But when Juan went to the authorities with all the information, Federal Police told him that according to their investigations, his brother was involved with some of the cartels so, he was a criminal who deserved it. Of course Juan defended his brother, and told them that even if that were true, they had the responsibility to investigate.

Juan continued insisting, until he was ordered to stop because "very important people" from Tampico were directly involved.

He realised this could affect him and his family.

He stopped insisting in Tampico, but he travels weekly to Mexico City, to a group of people whose families were taken.

They receive some group therapy and also legal advice on their claims. It is amazing the number of people who disappeared from 2009 to June 2013 around 24,800 people.

Just to give an example officially 1,200 people in Coahuila, unofficially, 1,100 in Nuevo Leon. Tamaulipas does not have an official or unofficial statistic, but is the state with the biggest amount of disappeared people

There is another friend, whose husband was taken in 2010, she also paid, but up to date, she hasn't seen her husband again.

She knows he is dead.

As responsible parents, they had contracted a life insurance, but she had not been able to claim on it, as there is no body.

Another friend of my husband told him that his brother had been taken, in Ciudad Mante, the Northeast of Tampico.

The family (wife, sons, brothers, nephews and nieces) asked loans, sold properties and gave their savings to get the money.

When they had part of the ransom, they hired a man to hand it over, as they were afraid to be taken, too.

That man told them that he was ordered to buy a prepaid mobile phone, and they called him there to give the instructions.

He was ordered to drive to Ciudad Mante, the kidnapers used to call him every 10 or 15 minutes, to know him where he was and giving him instructions. He was ordered to go near ciudad Mante, also to a path when he got there, it was dark.

They were waiting for him, he couldn't see anything, because they asked him to turn off the lights, and drove in the dark for a kilometer or two, until they asked him to stop.

They ordered to turn on and off the lights three times to know that it was him.

After he did it they lit a spotlight that blinded him for a few minutes. Immediately, they asked him to drive back. They ordered again to turn on and off the lights three times, and once again, was blinded by spotlights. They did it another three or four times, I guess to keep him helpless and afraid in order to control him.

Finally, they told him to put the money at a specific place, and leave.

They would call later to inform where they would release the man. Of course, the kidnapped man hasn't come back to his house yet.

There were rumors that he had been seen on an area between Ciudad Victoria and Mante apparently working as "hawk".

One of the nieces worked in The Bajío (lowlands) in a region of central Mexico, and talked about his uncle with her boss.

Her boss was an important business woman, who had bodyguards from Europe, she told her to talk to her bodyguards.

If they agreed to help her, it was ok for the boss.

She did it, and the bodyguards told her that they had been trained to search and rescue people in that kind of situation and gave her their fee. The fee also included to kill everyone involved in the kidnapping, to avoid or minimize the risk of revenge. If the man was alive, they would bring him to the family, if he was dead, they would recover the body. She immediately contacted her family but after talking about it, they decided not to pay for it.

They just gave up.

The family was afraid to be involved in endless spiral of extortion and violence. What if the bodyguards would turn against them? After all, zetas began as a group hired by the Mexican government, trained to protect people, (with our money!! the money of our taxes!!) and now they were using their knowledge against citizens.

Once again, it was not like in the movies, it wouldn't be like Denzel Washington in "Man on fire" or any other similar movies like "Taken", where the good guy kills every bad guy and rescues the victim.

It was not that easy. They were just ordinary people susceptible to be corrupted.

My opinion on Mexican Politicians, and government workers, I am SICK to know about corruption at every level, from the bottom to the top.

When I won the trial against my ex-husband to get my girls' passports, I was astonished because my ex-husband was arrested so fast.

(He hadn't given money for their expenses and refused to pay).

It usually takes years in Mexico just to find the people, and some more years to arrest them!

But he was found very fast.

The police officers requested us money to arrest him, ($2,000 a very low rate as they used to request some more) and my lawyers told me that now the mafia was responsible to arrest people involved in felony prosecution, (to get bigger fees) and police officers were just in charge of misdemeanor prosecutions and their fee has to be lower.

Later, I knew that police officers told my ex-husband that I had paid them to punch him and if he didn't want to be punched, the fee had to paid, (also $2,000).

I didn't ask this of course, but he paid.

This situation was convenient to me because I got passports faster, but I wonder, who are we going to ask for help, if there is corruption at every level?

It seems that the more I investigate; the worse is the scenario I find. I love my country, but the system sucks.

Despite this, wherever I turn around me I find people that had survived violence and corruption. Amazing histories, of courage and dignity. I just can believe that we are in the hands of God, because our governors haven't helped us and probably they won't do it.

Diana

May 2013

We went to Poza Rica, in the south of Tampico in the state of Veracruz. My husband has some family in there, and it was the wedding of one of his nieces. As the city is so small, people who can do it, used to send their kids to study high school and college in Tampico, Veracruz or Mexico City. The older son in the family has two kids, a 24 year old girl and a boy also in his 20s. During 2010, the boy was in Tampico, and was taken from the street by zetas. They called his father, and asked him for a big amount of money. His father works as head of safety, answering directly to the a very important politician in Veracruz.

He was ordered to go to the HEB supermarket in Hidalgo Avenue to pay the ransom for his son.

When he got there, they took him too and made him lie on the vehicle's floor.

He could see billboards, and guessed where he was been driven. He said they were just 3 or 4 blocks of distance, just before he got to the house where he was held captive with his son.

We could assume that they were in the north of the city, where Avenida Hidalgo becomes Carretera Tampico-Mante.

He says that a whole family (with kids) was responsible for them. Kids were directly involved in that work, they were part of it, and they (the kids) acted like if it were something normal. While they were there, they were beaten, and tortured. To push the family to pay faster, his son was taken outside the house, and was seated on an ant's nest for hours.

He could hear the screams of his son and he couldn't help him. The boy spent two nights sleeping in the yard.

His body was fully covered with ants' bites.

As the father worked for the government the army was looking for him.

He believes that the army was close to finding the house, because zetas ordered him to call his family and ask the army to stop the search or they would kill them.

They were three days and two nights in that house, because his family was able to pay the ransom quickly. But there were more people in that house, people that had been there for weeks in the same conditions as they were.

They haven't come back to Tampico, only hearing the name of the city literally causes them goose bumps.

They do not understand why we are still here. We told them we have learned to live with it. It is safer now, not as it used to be, but safer. We live our daily life with a low profile. Our cars are not showy, our clothes are not fancy, and our social life is restrained to the minimum.

Unfortunately, small towns around Tampico, are now suffering the cockroach effect. They are now going through the same thing we went through some months ago.

Their girls are taken from the streets and used for sexual purposes. They are lucky if they are released alive. The boys are caught to work for zetas, as cannon fodder.

It is ironic, 5 years ago I used to pray and thank God because in Mexico we could live peacefully, because children could live as children, with no worries.

I used to be sad when I listened about kids in Africa that were taken from their houses to fight in wars that do not belong to them. Now we are living the same.

What does He (God) want me to learn? To depend upon him? To thank every day of my life as it comes, just because we are alive? That our lives are not in our hands?

Or maybe, that we are strong enough to go through this? Maybe my responsibility as a mother?

That I should educate my kids so they do not become monsters like the zetas?

Well, we have done it. We have learned a lot. My kids, my three kids are safe up until now, How long are they going to be safe?

My grandmother used to say to us, "Things that don't kill you, make you stronger." So, are we stronger now?

We haven't been killed.

So I guess we are stronger.

Diana

Luz María Dávila

During my last vacations, I saw a movie about a woman whose son had died from malaria in Africa, and she found a relief for her pain, by proposing that the government in the USA donated mosquito nets to people who lived in places with high risk of infection.

It was a nice movie, and probably, in other countries you have a voice that can be heard. You can find a relief to your pain by turning your son's death in to something positive for other people.

But in Mexico it is dangerous. We have no voice; we have never ever had a voice, because corruption affects every part of the government.

Since I was a child, I have known about people who have been killed by the government, because their claims affected the government's interests. We just need to remember Tlatelolco in 1968.

If someone is brave enough to claim for justice, then they are persuaded to stop investigating or pushing, because important people are involved (usually politicians, or their relatives).

If you don't, you can be killed.

There are three examples of people who claimed in national and sometimes international media, for justice, in the last three years.

Two of them are still alive.

On January 30, 2010 in the neighborhood Villas de Salvarcar, in Júarez, Coahuila, 16 people were brutally murdered while they were in a house, celebrating the 18th birthday of a boy.

Most of them were students from local high schools and college , their ages were from 14 to 20 years old.

Most of them lived in the same neighborhood, and their parents were at home, just a few meters away.

Gloria Moreno´s home is just next to the house where the boys were killed. She remembers in detail the most terrifying night of her life. "I heard a loud noise, just as if some pieces of metal were falling, people screaming and then, silence, followed by three detonations, when I went outside, there were people on the floor, covered with blood.

I looked inside the house, there was slaughter. I had met most of the people in the house, I could recognize them by the clothes and shoes they were wearing."

Authorities said to the media, that a group of hired killers had got to that house in four pickups and shot people inside.

As Juarez had been the scene of drug wars for two years, they assumed that the people in the house were involved with some drug cartel or other. It was also a way to dismiss the incident, and eventually, let people forget it, and not do anything at all.

As usually happens.

I saw the video of Luz María Dávila for the first time, because a friend sent it to me by e-mail, in 2010, with the headline "Those are balls".

I remember that the first line I heard her say was "I am not going to go back to my chair, I am not afraid, because I have nothing to lose, I've already lost my children. I am not going to be quiet, because I am telling the truth".

She had been followed by the members of the president's staff, who tried to take her back to her chair, so she couldn't speak the truth. It wasn't until the president told them, "Let her", speak", that she began her unforgettable speech.

"Excuse me, Mr. President, but I will not shake your hand because you are not my friend. I cannot welcome you, because as far as I am concerned, you are not welcome here...no one is..."

After ignoring the members of the president's staff, the short woman in a blue sweater proceeded to reprimand President Felipe Calderon and then the mayor and the governor also.

She complained: "This Ferriz and this Baeza, they always say the same things over and over, but they don't do anything, it is worse Mr. President.

And for me, there is no justice. I want you to put yourself in my place... what do you think I am feeling right now?

All I have are two dead sons. And I only had two sons, At home we are still praying the novena for them. "Then, she turned around and faced the media.

"Why don't you say anything sirs? But you were here, cheering the President, because he came? Yes, good, but I want you to put yourself in my place." She turned to face the President again.

She was Luz Maria Dávila, resident of Villas de Salvarcar who lost her only two sons—Marcos, 19, and Jose Luis Piña, 17—on Saturday, January 30, 2010.

Face to face with Calderon in the Cibeles Convention Center, Mrs Dávila demanded an apology from him for having called the boys gangsters.

"It is not fair that my boys are at a party and are killed. I want you to apologize for what you said that they were gangsters.

It is a lie!

One of them was in preparatory school and the other was at the University of Chihuahua.

They were not hanging out in the streets!

Because my boys didn't have... They didn't have... It is just that I cannot believe it, I can't believe what you had said about them, they didn't have time to hang out in the streets! They were studying and working."

Mrs. Dávila made her statement in front of the government officials and some 600 people gathered at the meeting of the authorities with representatives of the Juárez community.

"I want the Juárez we had some years ago, not the violent Juárez we have now, because Juárez is in mourning.

Here in Juárez for two years they have been committing these murders and they have been committing many other crimes and no one does anything about it.

I am only asking that justice be done, not only for my two children, but for everyone," she added. "Because in that party, there were other students that were 14 years old. It was a party, for a student's 18th birthday.

From his place on the presidium, Calderon only managed to say to her, "but of course."

But the grieving mother did not accept this.

"Don't you tell me 'but of course.' DO SOMETHING! If it were you who had had your son murdered, you would not leave any stone unturned. Literally, you would be looking under the rocks for the killers, but since I don't have any resources, I am not able to look for them..."

The auditorium broke into applause and Luz Maria Dávila into tears.

A woman stood up to console her as she walked back to her seat where she had been since the beginning of the meeting with representatives of community organizations, in front of the reporters covering the event.

Dávila's speech completely destroyed what was left of the already deteriorating decorum of the President's four-hour meeting with different sectors of the Juárez society.

Luz Maria then took a seat in a corner of the room.

While a visibly upset Margarita Zavala de Calderon, the President's wife, stood at her husband's side so that she could see where Mrs. Dávila was, still crying, her face in her hands and surrounded by others.

The First Lady then left the stage and approached Dávila, hesitating and raising her head to try to see through the crowd surrounding her.

Mrs. Calderon finally got close enough to embrace Dávila and spoke with her for a few minutes. Dozens of reporters tried to capture the moment with their recorders and cameras.

Mrs. Dávila's appearance in front of the stage came as a complete surprise.

Governor Jose Reyes Baeza was just finishing his speech, saying that he was primarily responsible for what happened in Chihuahua. Meanwhile, the General Secretary of the Government (Gomez Mont) left the room in response to the complaint that young demonstrators were being beaten outside the convention center.

Dávila had remained silent for more than an hour and a half, accompanied by activists, including the actress Perla de la Rosa, seated on one side of the large room that had been rented for the meeting.

When she had arrived and answered questions from the media, Mrs. Dávila said that she was there because she had not wanted to speak in private with the president in Casa Amiga, that she had waited for him in the park at Villas de Salvárcar, in the spot where her two sons had been shot and killed.

When the event began with President Calderon's speech, Dávila stood up in place and along with six other women, turned her back to the president while he spoke.

They were relating what he had said to the other victims' families.

The President said: "I also told them that I understood perfectly their upset, their irritation, the misunderstanding that could have led to the declarations that we made at first, when questioned by the press. I told them that the initial investigations were carefully guarded.

I indicated precisely, the power, that these initial inquiries were leading to, that according to the first declarations of the first person who was arrested.

That it had to do with aggression from one criminal group towards another rival group and that this led precisely to a misunderstanding and a stigmatization," said the president.

"But whatever might have been the meaning of my words, I told these parents that I presented to them and that I offered them my most heartfelt apologies if any of my words had offended them or their children's memory," he added.

However, nothing that he said would persuade Dávila and the rest of the demonstrators to turn around and face the President, not even pressure from members of the presidential staff who approached them and asked them to sit down.

The women responded that they were not going to move.

The protestors only sat down when Calderon finished his speech and one hour and a half later, Mrs. Dávila decided to directly reproach the president, just at the moment when the crowd was applauding Governor Jose Reyes Baeza.

After she made her statement and after various officials offered their consolation by standing to embrace her, Mrs. Dávila left the building quietly, wiping away her tears.

Davila's speech shook society all over Mexico, and also got the public's attention of the Juarez situation in a way that no other person or institution had done before. It was evident that there was corruption inside local governments, and they were forced to act accordingly

A month later, Calderón launched the program "Todos Somos Juaréz", and the federal government donated 400 million pesos to the city to repair the social damage.

Part of that money was used to finance and renew parks in Villa de Salvarcar which used to be only empty lots covered with grass and trash. Also, a baseball field, a library, and a sports unit were built. But Davila is not able to enjoy them. "I am happy because some other kids will play in these places, but I cannot avoid thinking that they were built with the blood of my kids, and their friends.

Why did they wait until those kids were killed? We already had these needs before."

By July, 2011, four people were found guilty of the murders. Juan Alfredo Soto Arias, Aldo Fabio Hernández Lozano, José Dolores Arroyo Chavarría and Heriberto Martínez.

This was something amazing. In Mexico it usually takes years just to arrest criminals, and it is almost impossible to get a fair trial.

By the end of July, 2011, José Antonio Acosta Hernández, leader of Cartel de Juarez, was arrested and later he declared that he had ordered the attack because he had been told that in the house there were members of "Artistas Asesinos" (Assassin Artists) a group that supported Joaquín El Chapo Guzmán.

It was a mistake. In the party, there were AA members, but they were members of a football team from the local high school whose age group was represented by the initials AA.

Five of them were in the party, only two survived. When hired killers got there, they realized that the people they were looking for were not there and they were facing unarmed students.

But they opened fire anyway.

Israel Arzate Melendez, a suspect in the murders, was arrested in 2011, while he was driving a jeep that was reported as stolen.

He was identified by 11 witnesses as a participant in the Villa de Salvarcar Murders.

He is under house arrest, in the same neighborhood where witnesses live. Despite all this evidence, he has not been judged yet. His defending counsel got a "order de amparo" (injunctive relief and antisuit injunction) because he argues that he was tortured to confess.

The National Commission on Human Rights (CNDH in Spanish), the UN, and other national and international organizations are requesting his exoneration. Giving him more rights to the criminal rather than the victims. (This only happens in Mexico!)

I personally believe this is not real justice.

However in this country, the arrest and prosecution of 5 of 6 criminals gives us some relief and a sense of justice.

It wouldn't be possible without Davila´s courage.

When you have nothing to lose, because everything you have has been taken away, all you have left is your voice, to claim for justice.

Near to the house where those kids were killed, there is a lot of graffiti. One piece is especially impressive.

It says, **"Let the walls speak what bullets keep in silence. My country has abandoned me"**.

Diana

Reynosa 2010 and 2013

In Reynosa, lives a close friend of my mother, that we call Aunt Sofia, even though she is not our aunt.

She is married to a Seventh Day Adventist minister, and some of his own kids (now all of them adults) belong to that religion. So, even if they live in a dangerous neighborhood in Reynosa, nobody messes with them, due to their religion.

Somehow, she created a world apart to bring up their kids, without discriminating against the other kids in the neighborhood.

They used to play together, and now most of his own kids are hard working, responsible adults.

They are still known in the neighborhood as "the brothers or sisters" according to their gender, because they usually call each other this way in church.

She is some kind of mother for everybody in neighborhood. Anyone who has a problem, can go the her house to get a cup of coffee and also get advice, comprehension, help or a scolding full of swearing. She is a whole Mexican matriarch.

My husband and my dad used to stay in her house very often when they traveled to Reynosa. They could stay in a hotel, but they preferred aunt's Sofia house, because they were always welcome.

One day, they were getting ready to sleep, but as it was a cold night, they opened the closet trying to get a blanket.
There were some blankets in the upper part of the closed, so my husband tried to pull them down but they were too heavy. He got a chair, and took a look in there, and found out that the blankets were wrapping some AK47 rifles.

Next day they talked about it with Aunt Sofia. She told them that one of her neighbors had asked her to keep them in her house for a few days. She knew it was wrong, but she knew the police would never look for them in her house.

Everybody knew her house would be the last house in the neighborhood where police would expect to find weapons. "I know it is dangerous" she said "but I just couldn't say nothing, I have known that guy since he was a kid, I don't want him to go to jail."

After that incident, my father and husband decided no longer stay in her house.

But they still visit her sometimes when they are in Reynosa.

She has been living in the same neighborhood for almost 40 years.

She met each one of the guys while they grew up with her own children, and later on, with her grandchildren.

Near her house, there was a family of well known retail drug dealers.

It was a "family business", everybody in this house participated selling drugs even though they had the chance to get another kind of job.

The youngest boy in this family, Pepe used to be a pickpocket too. My dad and husband met him when they stayed with Aunt Sofia some months during a job. He showed him the way he could take the wallet from their pockets just before them, without them noticing it.

Of course, he gave them back the wallets. It seemed that he considered my dad and my husband as his friends, because never tried to steal from them.

Pepe used to be protected by his father. Several times drug boys tried to take him from his house for his behavior against them, and all those times, his father used to face them with a gun. Pepe´s dad used to say; "I might be killed, but I will kill some of them first!"

In 2010, Pepe was in his early 20s.

He thought it was time to be "independent" so he leased a big house just next to his father's house and was responsible to receive big loads of marijuana and cocaine.

The drugs usually were in there for a few days, later on, somebody picked them up.

That year, Pepe decided it was time to begin his own business, in the last loading; he kept some packages for himself.

There was too much drugs in there!

If he took some of it to sell it, no one would notice it! Or at least, he thought no one would notice it.

One morning, Aunt Sofia was in her house alone. That was strange, because her house is usually full of people. She saw some pickups parked in front of his house, and as she had a small store outside her house, she went out to serve.

Aunt Sofia knew some of the guys in the pickups, they had lived in the neighborhood since they were kids, and they had played with her grandsons.

They got out of the truck and bought some tuna cans.

All of them were carrying guns. It is sad to say, but that was not unusual, as she knew that Pepe's family worked in drug business just in front of her house.

But not all of them went to Pepe's house.

Some of them stood there, and consumed cocaine, using the tuna cans to sniff it. That morning, there was only Pepe in his house. His father had been sent out of the town for "business."

Most of the men went in to Pepe´s house, and two of them stood outside, by his door. Some stood with Aunt Sofia, and told her (politely, as they were the ones who knew her) –"Please, give us your mobile phone, and stay here, don't go to your house now".

By then, it was known that Pepe had taken some of the drugs, they did not want the drugs or money back, they wanted to give him a lesson, and warn to the other dealers what could happen to them if they attempt to do the same.

Pepe was cut into pieces when he was still alive, with an electric hand saw.

There is no poetry or romantic effect in this fact. It was not like in the movies, it wasn't funny and there was no black humor.

It was a human being cutting into pieces another human being.

There was no respect for human life. They did it in daylight, in a neighborhood full of people, and nobody did anything to stop it.

The men that did it, turned on the stereo, playing the music too loud, trying to suffocate the screams and the sound of the electric saw, but it was impossible, it was really impossible not to listen to them.

Aunt Sofia said she didn't know what to do. She just stared at the guys who were with her, and they just looked at her and shook their heads, as if they were telling her "No, you can't do anything".

She expected that someone else called the police or army, but nobody did it (it wouldn't help anyway, usually police are involved in the drug business).

At that moment she was not afraid to be hurt or killed, she just kept thinking "it is not true, it is not real."

She couldn't believe that something so terrible was going on in front of her house and to someone she knew.

Denial, blessed denial, in psychology means that someone denies that something has happened or is happening although he or she really knows it is true. Usually this happens because admitting it would cause a lot of pain.

Sometimes it helps you to go through a shocking situation when you are helpless, when your hands are tied and you cannot do anything.

But once you accept it really happened, reality beats you strongly and you have to build up your world, trying making every piece match again.

How do you build it up again?

How can you go on knowing that your perception of the world was wrong? Knowing that evil exists and it is closer to you than you had thought?

It is like if your ordinary life was a 100 pieces puzzle, but you have 25 more pieces; those 25 pieces are evil around you.

You know it is beautiful, perfect and complete with 100 pieces, but suddenly you have to include those 25 extra pieces and make it work, and you do not only have to make it work, you also have to make it look nice. Then, somehow we are able to go on.

I do not know if Pepe is the same guy who asked Aunt Sofia to keep the AK47 in her house. If so, probably he would be safer in jail. Or probably he would have been released with a darker heart.

Aunt Sofia does not like to talk about it, because it makes her feel sick, now that I am writing about it, it makes me feel sick too.

Did something similar happen to Agustin?

I had never thought before how he died. It was sad enough just to know that he has gone. Hope not! Oh God, Hope not! Hope he had just been shot in the head, and had had a quick death!

What kind of society are we if we have to choose between two evils to get some relief for a friend's death?

We know that Agustin was taken by zetas. Pepe used to work with the Cartel. None of them is better than the other.

Everything began as a war between zetas and cartels, but there was a moment when anyone with no respect for others and a gun, could do anything they wanted; because Tampico became a lawless city.

People began to have their parties locked in their houses, until some guys began to break in the parties to steal money, jewelry, cars, and rape the girls.

They knew there was a party because of the music and cars parked outside the house.

A woman that I know was celebrating her son's birthday at home. It was full of teenagers when these guys got there. Fortunately, the one who rape the girls was not "working" that day, so the girls in her house were not touched at all.

The army was not enough to control this mess.

They tried to help, but they were overwhelmed.

They are still overwhelmed.

My husband and my dad were stopped several times by the army to check their vehicles.

During an especially long trip, my dad got tired of being stopped at every checkpoint. An 8 hour trip became an 11 hour trip because they were checked at least 9 times.

The last time, one of the soldiers asked my dad if he was angry. "Of course I am angry," he replied. "My vehicle has been checked too many times from Tampico to here. You are not going to find anything new in this vehicle.

What is going on? Why are you just checking us? Is it the vehicle? Is it my face? There are other vehicles that are newer and better that this one and you do not stop them!"

"It is for your protection," the soldier told him.

"Protection?!!" said my dad. "We have been stopped also by the cartels and zetas, and you were not there! Some of my workers have been beaten and you did nothing to protect them! As soon as I leave this check point, I am on my own."

"Well," the soldier answered hesitating, "we are just doing our job"

"And you should let me do mine. It supposed I should have been in Morelia three hours ago!"

At that moment, my husband told my dad, "it's ok, man, let's go." Once in the vehicle, my husband asked my dad not to be aggressive with the soldiers. It could be dangerous too. They might be arrested for arguing they tried to avoid the revision.

On the second week of May, 2013, The Regional Championship of Charreria was held in Reynosa, Tamaulipas.

People from the local Lienzo, went there to participate. My husband and many of my friends belong to that lienzo. They were traveling in trucks to pull the trailers with the horses. There were at least 4 escaramuzas teams, with 8 horses each, and also two charros teams, with their own horses, and their baggage that includes their uniforms, saddles and harnesses which are really bulky because for charreria saddles are really big and heavy. They were not able to drive fast, and they knew it, but thought it was safer to travel than in 2010. Most of the charros and escaramuzas from Tampico traveled there with their families to cheer them up.

Everything went well when they traveled from Tampico to Reynosa, but when they were coming back, some of them had "incidents".

They were sending each other text messages during the trip, to warn of any danger.

In one of the trucks, were my husband, with a nephew that got the nickname of Rana (frog), a young guy that charros used to call Broccoli (due to his curly hair) and a friend of the family called Antonio. And in the vehicles, were my nephew's girlfriend, Antonio's wife, Luis six pack (because he was always with a can of beer in his hand) and his daughter, who was 16. All of them are close friends of mine.

There is a part of the road from Reynosa to Tampico that is now especially dangerous. It is called "La recta de Reynosa". It is a 146 kilometers straight road that goes from Reynosa to San Fernando, where in April 2011, were found 193 dead corpses in a mass grave

Luis was driving through this road, when he got a phone call. Some kilometers ahead, the escaramuza teachers and their family had been shot because they refused to stop.
In their vehicle were the teachers' kids; a 6 year old girl, who belonged to the escaramuza team, and a 4 year old boy.

Surprisingly the guys who shot them didn't have a vehicle, so they were able to continue driving fast for some kilometers until his vehicle stopped, because the motor had bullets. Fortunately, it broke down near to an army check point.

So, when a new and fancy double cab truck ordered him to stop, he did it immediately. He had no choice. At this point it was the same danger to run away than to stop, and besides, Luis six pack knew he couldn't drive faster, because he was pulling the trailer.

As soon as he parked, he got out of the vehicle with what he thought would be a friendly expression on his face.
And walked directly to the pickup, trying to keep his hands visible, to show he was not armed.

When he got to the vehicle, he gave a handshake to the guys inside and had the chance to take a discrete and quick look inside. There were two guys in the truck

He told me later that "They had a lot of guns, rifles and bullets all over the seats, to be taken quickly.

hey were wearing cartridge belts on his chest. And what in that moment, seemed to be thousands of grenades, on the seat between them, probably there were just 8 or 10 of grenades, but fear made me think there were so much more."

This situation was extremely stressful to him, because he was with three women and he felt responsible for their safety. In 2010, we knew about women that were taken by zetas and later released after been raped for more than 20 guys.

Some of them were not able to overcome it and committed suicide.

The men in the truck asked him (politely and with no swearing at all!!) where he came from, where he went, and if the horses were racehorses. He explained that they came from the Regional Championship of Charreria, and that the horses were used to that discipline.

"Are they expensive?" they asked him.

"Right now, and after this trip, I guess they are not expensive horses, they are only hungry and tired horses" answered smiling.

"Horses for Charrería are not as expensive as racehorses."

"It is OK to us, but our boss wants to talk to you." they replied.

"Wait a minute." Just a few minutes later, another double cab truck got there. It was not as new and fancy as the first one.

Luis was asked to go to the other vehicle, and as soon as the window was opened, he saw also two men in it.

The boss was a white and tall man that has blue eyes. (That is not very common in Mexico).

The driver seemed to be Native American. There were no weapons in this vehicle, or at least, they were not visible.

The boss was holding a big foam cup with whisky; (Luis was able to identify the drink just by the scent). He asked him the same questions, and seemed to be interested in Charrería.

After a quick questioning, he was able to go. Luis already knew about the incident with the escaramuza teachers.

He asked, "What is the best way to go back to Tampico?"

After San Fernando, there are two roads to go to Tampico, one through Soto La Marina, which is now lonely and dangerous, and another through Ciudad Victoria, which people think it is safer. But our friends had been already shot in that road.

"Why?" The boss asked back. "Have you been stopped already?"

"No, I just wondered which the best way to go was."

The boss stared at him and told him, "We are zetas. Go through Ciudad Victoria, and you won't be bothered again"

Luis walked back to his truck when the boss told him: "Hey, Güero (blonde) you haven't seen me, and I haven't seen you ok?" After these words, he closed the window and left.

He went back to his truck, with the girls, feeling relief and surprise. He couldn't believe that they were stopped by zetas and released so easily, with no damage.

He immediately called my husband and other charros, to warn them about it. But fortunately, there were no more incidents.

Last Sunday, June 16 2013, there were another 4 firefights at noon in Tampico. It was Fathers' day, and there were too many people on the street.

A friend of mine was on the street, she was having lunch with his family, at a tacos stand, something very popular in Mexico, when it began.

There was no place to hide. They had to lie on the floor, and her youngest girl (she is 11 years old) was so terrified that she clung so strong on her blouse and she finally tore it off.

We had thought by now that it has stopped, but it doesn't, it hasn't stopped.

I am shocked just to think what this situation is doing in a whole generation of kids. How this is affecting their psyche.

Are they going to become a more violent generation?

Or will they be more responsible? As this is a social problem, and we all are part of society, we all have the responsibility to find a solution.

How?

Sometimes as adults we do not know how to manager fear, how are we going to teach kids to do it?

To give a little example, I have 18 students in my classroom; they are 11 or 12 years old now. 16 of them had been at least in one firefight in since 2010.

In 2010 they were 8 or 9 years old. From those 16, three of them also had a relative that was taken.

Only one was released.

Three of them saw people die on the street, one of them saw a man die in front of his face, while he was lying on the floor under his dad's truck, trying to protect himself from bullets.

He said that the man drop his gun and it fell very close to him. He took it and threw it away because was afraid to be shot if he was near to it.

Some other was in their school's yard during a firefight and principal shouted them to lie on the ground, but they were left alone! There were no teachers with them! (They were not in my school at that moment!).

Two of them were playing on the street with their friends and next moment they were looking for a place to hide. One of them was alone at home during the shots, he hid in the closet and took a knife with him; he thought he could use it to protect himself if someone broke in his house.

Another two were walking with their mom from the school to his home when the shots began.

There were soldiers all over the street, and against the instructions given to citizens, one of the soldiers ordered them to run while he covered them. In their innocence, they just remember how funny was to watch her mom running leading them to their home. (After all they had never seen her run before!) But once in their house, they spent 40 minutes in the bathroom, with the family dog, a Rottweiler. Just imagine two adults, two kids, and a Rottweiler lying on the floor in a small bathroom.

The father of another of my students was beaten because as he was driving a fancy pickup they thought he had money, and he didn't. This is a small sample taken from my classroom.

How many kids in the city have been shocked by violence and fear?

Somewhere in Louisiana

A man who had the courage to denounce the links between some authorities in Tamaulipas and criminals organizations 15 years ago, is still awaiting justice.

He demands to the Mexican Federal Authorities that they stop impunity, and work with accuracy and objectivity on a migration warning launched on three ex- governors of Tamaulipas; Manuel Cavazos Lerma, Tomás Yarrington and Eugenio Hernández.

Omar Duran Perales went through really hard events that finally made him leave Mexico and request political asylum in the United States.

It is proof of how criminal organizations took control of the state, with the help of government officials at different levels, until everything went beyond their control.

It turned into the violence we have nowadays on the streets.

Omar Durán worked as Director of sanitary inspection in Tamaulipas. He witnessed the way some government officials quickly made agreements with drugs and weapons dealers.

Though he had the courage to denounce, he is not able to come back to Mexico, impunity on criminals kept him away and there are no authorities that can guarantee his safety. He holds on to hope, that some day, his individual rights will be respected, and he will be able to come back, with his family, to his home town.

Meanwhile, the politicians and government officials involved are still free.

The evidence that Omar presented, got a public prosecutor murdered, two agents who were "bought" by the cartels, one from the Attorney General in Mexico (PGR) and the other from Centre for Research and National Security (CISEN) and threats on his family by the governor of Tamaulipas of that time, Manuel C.

When Manuel Cavazos Lerma won the elections in 1992, the veterinarian Omar Durán, was invited to work as deputy director at sanitary inspection in Tamaulipas. Duran had met Manuel Cavazos Lerma, and his father a long time before he became governor.

Durán was responsible for inspecting every sanitary check point at every border of the state, At the south with Veracruz, at the north, with the United States, and to the west, with the state of Nuevo Leon.

There was a whole net of roads to inspect every farming product transported between Mexico and the United States. Omar was particularly surprised to find lorries carrying oranges from Veracruz to Nuevo Leon. To him it was like carrying "water to the river", as it is well-known that Nuevo Leon is the main orange producer in Mexico.

That was the first revelation to him. When he inspected one of those lorries, he found marihuana hidden among the oranges.

For his dedication Durán soon became an expert on detecting livestock with health problems and was promoted to Director for livestock farming.

In 1995, he got a phone call from a guy who identified himself as "Pedro". Pedro used to give him very detailed instructions to identify lorries that transported livestock in irregular situations.

Durán, in time, learned to trust Pedro, as every time he called him, everything he stated, was fulfilled just the way Pedro had said it would happen.

That way, Pedro showed him, which vehicles transported something more than just livestock. Durán discovered with the help of Pedro, that drug dealers often transport capsules with cocaine inside the animals.

The capsules are 10 cm. length.

With the information given by Pedro, and as Livestock farming director, Durán intercepted one of the lorries Pedro talked about.

Durán informed Enrique González, about it. He was an agent from CISEN, in Ciudad Victoria, the capital of the state.

As expected, no reclaim was made by the owners of the truck or animals, due to the nature of the load.

When the hours went by, livestock inspectors and Enrique González, witnessed that the animals died.

This as consequence of the cocaine capsules that exploded inside them.

Pedro kept informing Durán about other drug loads that were carried in livestock, while Durán intercepted them always requesting the assistance of PGR to seize the drugs and inform agent Enrique González from CISEN, what was going on. Until, González (yes, the agent!) warned Durán to stop intercepting drug loads.

The reason that González gave "This is something that nor Durán, or CISEN or anybody would be able to stop".

One day, Pedro called Durán to inform him about a lorry that was transporting around 40 cattle from Texas to the south of Mexico, and it would go through San Fernando, a small city close to the border with Texas.

Pedro assured that there were rifles hidden in the lorry. Durán, as director of sanitary inspection, called his workers and gave instructions to intercept any vehicle with characteristics previously described.

Some hours later, the inspectors called back, to tell him they had intercepted a lorry, with around 40 cows, from Alice, Texas, with the destination of the states of Morelos and Chiapas, in Mexico.

The owner of the truck, was Raul Ruiz Ruiz, a rich cattle breeder from Texas.

Omar Durán drove from Ciudad Victoria, to San Fernando and checked the vehicle himself. At the ends of the cage, covered with manure and hay, there were two packages, wrapped with jute and tape. Each package had 20 rifles.

With the shipment stopped, Durán called Enrique González, to let him know about the weapons, according to the instructions he got from the agent.

González told him he would request instructions from Main Offices in México City and would let him know, next morning, what he should do. González called next morning to tell him that the best option was to let the truck go, to minimize any risk to him or the inspectors. The Agent also explained that they would stop the vehicle some kilometers ahead.

Some hours later, González gave a call Durán because they were not able to find the truck, despite the road from the border to San Fernando is a 146 km. straight line.

Nobody ever knew what happened with the rifles, the truck or even the cattle. No claim was made on the lorry on behalf of Raul Ruiz Ruiz, a rich, cattle breeder from Texas.

From that moment, Durán never trusted agent González again.

For two years, Inspector Durán witnessed, intercepted and denounced drugs and arms trafficking, but the only thing he got in return was threats.

From 1995 to 1997 he requested assistance from state and federal authorities, and gathered evidence to arrest drugs dealers and arms traffickers, Until September 11, 1997, when the Governor, Manuel Cavazos Lerma, threatened him.

The daughters of Durán, who were 5 and 10 years old at that time, attended the same school with the kids of the governor. One day, the older girl got home in a panic and told him that the driver of the governor had given her a message "Tell your dad that if he does not close his mouth, we are going to take both of you".

The love for his daughters, and his desire to protect them, made him go to the governor's house, and face him with the things his driver had told them.

Deep inside, Durán still had the hope that everything was nothing but a misunderstanding.

But the governor, did not apologize or scold his driver. He just answered that Durán should not worry about his daughters during school time –there were too many people to attempt to do anything. But the worse was, when the governor told him, that Durán was the only one responsible for these threats; he should accept the benefits this knowledge could give him. After all, the drug business had enough money for everyone.

Durán drove back home furious, but still believing they would not do anything against his family. Trying to calm down, he watered his garden, when a pick up, with the logo of Tamaulipas Government, parked by his house and got out a man, who asked him if he was Durán.

When he nodded, the man told him:

"Look at this face, because tonight, I am going to come back to kill your daughters".

Durán faced him, and challenged him to fight with him, as all the problem was among adults.

But the guy just told him again; "Tonight, I will come back for your daughters."

Durán and his wife packed just a few personal things, and drove, with their kids for three hours from Cd. Victoria, to the border with the United States, where they requested political asylum. Probably, those were the three longest hours in his life.

Migration agents, put them in touch with DEA and FBI agents, who warned them, that they had to check first, if what they had said was true.

Some hours later, they confirmed that armed men broke into Duran´s house and had destroyed everything they had left behind..Then, and only then, were they allowed to enter the USA.

Omar Durán already knows who gave the order to destroy his house.

After all, he was threatened by the governor himself. He claims he has the right to live in his own country, as any Mexican citizen, with his family, in his house, under the protection of the authorities.

He has been trying to come back for 15 years, but there is no authority who guarantee he will be safe. José Patiño Moreno, Director of Special Prosecutor in Crimes Against Health from PGR was the only one brave enough to open an investigation and is now dead

In 2000, Patiño, his two assistants, and also Oscar Pompa Plaza, special prosecutor, and Rafael Torres Bernal, Captain from the Mexican Army vanished on the street of Tijuana. When the bodies were found, by the Patiño's car, that was destroyed, a police officer said, that trying to carry the bodies, was like carrying sacks filled with ice cubes.

Their heads had been crushed with a press, and almost every bone in their body were broken. Local police, probably, paid by the mafia, insisted they had died in an "unfortunate car accident".

Some years later, when the Arellano-Felix cartel lost control on the north west of Mexico, two police commanders were accused of the murders of Patiño and the people who were with him.

Unfortunately, everything points that the investigation open on Duran accusations, died with Patiño in 2000.

Despite the evidence presented against him, Manuel Cavazos Lerma served as Secretary of Electoral Action, for the PRI, (Instutional Revolutionary Party) in 2011.

This was when Peña Nieto served as governor in the State of Mexico.

He now serves as senator of the republic, representing LXII legislature.

His campaign as senator, was fully supported by Peña Nieto, during a political meeting held on February 2nd. 2012 in Cd, Victoria, Tamaulipas. By that time, everybody already knew about the evidence and investigation against him.

Oran's Dictionary of the Law (1983) defines treason as:

"...[a]...citizen's actions to help a foreign government overthrow, make war against, or seriously injure the [parent nation]." In many nations, it is also often considered treason to attempt or conspire to overthrow the government, even if no foreign country is aiding or involved by such an endeavor.

Isn't it treason when someone who is serving the nation acts this way? Isn't it worse, when the actions comes from people who should protect us? They are betraying what they represent.

Diana & Lance

2010- 2011

During 2010 at the American School we met Lance Manley. He was teaching my daughter Elizabeth English. The first time I talked to him, was because she didn't finish her class work. She hadn't done anything at all that day!

So I was there, wishing the Earth would open under my feet and swallow me! I thought, "Great ! It is the first time I talk with her teacher, and he is already complaining about her! And we have witnesses!"

He was with his supervisor. Lance told me that he was frustrated because my daughter was a good student, so he asked her to do the class work as homework.

That changed Elizabeth's attitude.

Due to ADHD (which we didn't know she had) every teacher had complained about her in High School, but nobody had told her she was good at anything...until Lance.

She was happy with the English lessons. She used to tell me that Lance looked just like her younger sister, (with glasses and long, curly hair) and that he had told her she laughed like a baby. She liked that, so after the first embarrassing meeting, everything went well.

Before Lance left we had a parents meeting. His supervisor was there again. Lance told us that he wouldn't accept the kids to his Facebook, because he was a 40 year old man, with nothing in common with the kids. As he had been a police officer in England, he knew it was not proper to do it. We were amazed .

He had nothing in common with the kids?!!

He had been teaching them for months! If he left, how would the kids keep in touch with him? We wanted –or at least I wanted- that my daughter could know another way of living. Broaden her horizons, I wanted her to know that life was not only violence and fear. Lance seemed surprised but said if we thought it was OK then he would accept our kids as friends on Facebook.

The last day of classes, Elizabeth got out of the classroom with a big smile on her face. She showed me a certificate, that Lance had made for her. There was a baby girl seated laughing on a shopping cart (I do not remember what it said) but she told me, "Look what teacher Lance gave me! Isn't it funny?" She placed it in a special notebook for months.

That was the last time we saw him in Tampico.

Epilogue To 2nd Edition
April 2014

Things are getting worse. We were OK for a few months, but now, violence is again on the streets. After El Chapo was arrested the cartels are fighting again to get the supremacy, and now they are not discrete.

Right now, that I am writing these lines, there is a firefight outside my house, right now. I went downstairs to the laundry, and heard them. My girls are upstairs, at home, don't know if I should stay downstairs, or go upstairs with them. I have told them to go to the restroom if they hear gun fire.

I Finally decided go upstairs, and my two girls are at the door, waiting for me to close it. My Great Dane follows me and we get in to the house. The French window is open, and we are afraid that somebody can break in the house, so, Elizabeth closes the window. Luisa and I run to close the windows so we can set the alarm on. Then we go to the restroom. They are so close! It seems they are just outside.

I can hear them by the window! They are everywhere around the house! We have our mobile phones and I call my husband, to warn him and ask him to be careful, he is in a town close to Tampico, and my son is out, with my nephew and his wife.

So Lupe, my second daughter, calls my nephew to let him know about it and asks him to go directly to his house. They are in downtown. And Elizabeth calls a friend of hers who had just left the house some minutes ago. My hands are shaking, but I manage to send a message to Lance lol, don't know why, but I did it.

Then minutes later, they leave. We can hear the fire in the distance. My husband calls me and tells me that they, "the bad guys", are now close to my parents' house. He had called my nephew and asked him to go to a supermarket, and stay there until he can pick up my son.

When my son gets home later, he tells me he had to run from my nephew's car to HEB, because the soldiers were chasing some pickups on Hidalgo Avenue.

There were not shootings, but they can hear the sirens and didn't want to be on the street, just in case. He knows about the firefight near our house.

Some friends text me, one of them is in her mother's house, and now she cannot go back home. The army have closed the street. Another tells me that they were coming back from the charreada, and saw two pick-ups chasing and shooting each other. There is a third one that tells us that now the firefight is in a neighborhood called Tancol, it is next to mine, but far enough to not hear the shooting.

One of my friends, that is texting me, tells me that some members of Cartel del Golfo want to form their own cartel and killed the brother of the Chief of Cartel del Golfo in Tampico.

Great! Now we have golfos vs golfos, and golfos vs zetas! Two of them were enough, now there are three!

What I wanted to tell you, is that now, in La Herradura, the club where my husband trains, there is a member of cartel del golfo.

Actually, he is the chief I mentioned a few lines above. He has a low profile, his car or clothes are expensive, but not showy. Everything seems to be ok, he does not mess with anybody. The charros know about him. What he does for a living. He is not arrogant. He is not humble either. They think he just wanted a place where he can have some kind of normality in his life. A place where he could go, take a drink and talk with someone who is not involved in the drug business.

He does not mess with anybody. But two weeks ago, he allowed some of his workers, (mercenaries and drug dealers) to spend the day in La Herradura, with his jet ski.

The same day we went there.

When I got there, with my girls, and their friend, my husband told me "I came first, and they came later, but I cannot ask them to leave, and if we leave, they may take it as an offense.

It could be worse. Remember all those stories we have listened about.

Just tell the girls to do not take off their shorts and t-shirts . Don't let them wear their bikinis, I do not want any problem with them".

Their boss was not there, he just drove them and left.

We spent the afternoon, pretending we were having fun, but waiting for the right moment to leave. I did not like the way one of them stared at Sammy. One the of women who was with them told me he has brain damage for consuming drugs. It doesn't make me feel better. And also, I am worried for the friend of my girls, I invited her, it is my responsibility!

Finally after three hours, we left.

At home my husband told us that the other woman, was actually a 16 years old girl, minor according to Mexican laws. She looked older, probably because she was overweight. While we were there, she invited a friend, another little girl who did not tell her mother where she was. They were driving a jet ski, and fell off into the water. As those girls had drank a lot, were not able to get back on the Jet Ski. They did not have swimsuits on, were wearing jeans, t-shirts and sneakers.

While the girls were in the water, they were wondering what they would say to their mothers, how would they explain their soaking clothes. Their mothers didn't know where they were, or who was with them.

What if they would leave them there? Their mother knew they were together but in another place. Probably the girls were mesmerized for the money, or the jet ski, probably they thought they could get some benefit from them. But they were just little girls playing with fire.

Last week I went with my husband to a charreada. It was also the birthday party of a charro, and he invited us. We were sitting on a table, and our husbands were on another next to us. So, the people who don't know us, would think we were alone.

The charros had to leave the room to take care of the horses, and 20 or 30 minutes after they left, we also stood up to go out. There was a table by the door, with two men sitting at it.

As one of them is a friend of my husband, I said good bye to him and also to the men who was on the table with him. But the one I didn't know, undressed me with his eyes. I was astonished, everybody knows me in that club, and any of my husband's friend would do that, to any of us. It doesn't matter if they find us attractive or not. They wouldn't do it for respect to our husbands. I stared at him, not challenging him, but just be sure if I've seen what I've seen. He stared at me, and did it again.

I turned around and left the room, still more astonished than angry. Once outside, I asked to a friend, "¿Who was with Don Mode? "

"Didn't see, why?"

"He scanned me" (a Mexican way to say he undressed me with his eyes).

My friend turned around, to check who was that man and told me in a low voice "That was the Chief of the Tampico!" we both knew what she meant.

There was another charreada today, but I didn't want to go, I stood at home with my girls. Instead of being scanned by gangs, we had the firefight.

I don't know what is the worst.

There are rumours that the bad guys will shut down the power (they have done it before). And that tomorrow will be worse. My husband just came downstairs and asked us to turn off the lights. He got a message that worried him.

Our kids will sleep tonight in our bedroom.

34488206R00142

Made in the USA
Charleston, SC
10 October 2014